MICHIGAN BUSINESS PAPERS

Number 61

The Department of Economics of Western Michigan University is pleased to cooperate with the Division of Research at the Graduate School of Business Administration, The University of Michigan, in presenting this collection of papers in which six distinguished economists discuss the economic effects of multinational corporations internationally and on the economies of the host and home countries. This volume is the tenth in a series being published under these auspices.

MICHIGAN   BUSINESS
PAPERS   Number 61

The Economic Effects of Multinational Corporations

*Lectures given at Western Michigan University
under the sponsorship of the Department of
Economics, academic year 1974-75*

WERNER SICHEL, Editor

Published by the
Division of Research
In Cooperation with
The Program in International Business
Graduate School of Business Administration
The University of Michigan
Ann Arbor, Michigan

ISBN-0-87712-171-0

Copyright © 1975

by

The University of Michigan

CONTENTS

To
Beatrice
Larry and Linda

PREFACE

The term "multinational enterprise" is not new, but only in the last few years has it become a part of the popular language used by journalists and T.V. commentators. It often takes on sinister connotations—multinationals that actively engage in *sub rosa* plots to influence the outcome of elections in foreign countries, or multinationals that are alleged to be the real culprits responsible for our "energy crisis." While particular multinational corporations appear to have been guilty of more than mere indiscretions, it is incorrect to brand generally all multinational firms as world-wide troublemakers. The multinational enterprise is nothing more than a firm that owns resources—usually in the form of a subsidiary company—beyond its home borders. Just as advancements in transportation and communication technology have allowed firms to expand within their national boundaries, so, too, have they influenced international expansion. Understanding that managers of business firms attempt to maximize the present value of their enterprises leads us to expect that multinational business will grow when foreign investment opportunities appear to be more promising than those at home. This is what has happened. A list of the largest companies in the world today is practically identical to a list of the most influential multinational corporations. One needs only to examine *Fortune* magazine's list of "the Fifty Largest Industrial Companies in the World" (see, for example, *Fortune,* August 1974, p. 185) to find a virtual "who's who" in multinational corporations.

Having stripped multinational corporations of any fantasized characteristics, we set out to examine what, if any, unique economic effects they may have. This question is addressed in this volume by six distinguished economists: William James Adams, George H. Hildebrand, Harry Magdoff, G. C. Hufbauer, Gerhard Rosegger, and William G. Shepherd. Each was assigned a particular topic on the basis of his interest, research, and experience.

Our first author, Professor William James Adams, focuses on how multinational corporations affect the state of competition in national product markets. He begins by showing that multinationals can only come into being when the markets in both the source and the host country are less than perfect. Only when a source country firm has some fairly significant advantage over host country firms can it overcome some of the disadvantages inherent to foreign firms, such as unfamiliarity with customs, risk of expropriation, and communication difficulties. Likewise, sufficient competition among source country firms would ensure that they would license host country firms to use their technology or their brand names rather than engage in direct foreign investment. Having established that imperfect markets are a necessary prerequisite to firms' becoming multinational, Professor Adams addresses the question of whether the multinationals reduce or reinforce these imperfections. He suggests that the result depends on the extent to which multinationals recognize their mutual interdependence and how they effect entry barriers. The evidence which Professor Adams presents leads him to conclude that multinationals enhance international collusion and raise the barriers to entry. He therefore calls on governments to require multinationals to report in greater detail and suggests that governments stop providing incentives to multinationality. Further, Adams advocates an outright ban on international mergers or joint ventures involving leading firms.

In contrast, our second author, Professor George H. Hildebrand, considers the multinational to have a "constructive place in a worldwide system of private enterprise." He offers an explanation for the much greater amount of direct foreign investment by U.S. firms as compared to firms from other countries and examines the pattern of U.S. direct foreign investment both in terms of geography and major function. He finds manufacturing and extractive industries to be the most important functions, and Western Europe and Canada the most important areas. Hildebrand, whose primary interest is the effect on labor, is not convinced, however, that U.S. job-losses to these areas or to the third world countries is very great. He points out that some production by U.S. firms in foreign countries—chrome production, for example—involves no job losses, because of the inability to produce it in the United States. Also, few job-losses occur when the cost of producing the items is so much greater in the United States that production would of necessity be very limited.

Hildebrand argues that the U.S. employment loss to foreign workers that has occurred over the past twenty-five years cannot easily be laid at the feet of multinational corporations. He interprets the great growth of direct foreign investment by U.S. firms as merely an attempt by them to survive. The real culprit, as Hildebrand views it, has been U.S. government policy, which has promoted fixed foreign exchange rates, fostered inflation, and allowed substantial deficits in the U.S. international balance of payments.

The third paper in this volume is by Harry Magdoff, the co-editor of *Monthly Review*. His focus is on how we arrived at the "Age of the Multinational" and what effects it has had on the less developed countries of the world. Magdoff views the emergence of multinationals as just another stage in the fulfillment of the driving forces of capitalist enterprise—greater corporate sales and profits. In this context he provides what he believes are the main reasons for the "flowering of the multinationals after the Second World War." Likewise, he traces the relative surge of U.S.-based multinationals and offers several explanations for their post World War II prominence.

When examining what the effects of multinationals have been on third world nations, Magdoff distinguishes between what he calls the conservative, liberal, and radical views surrounding this question. Conservatives argue that, while multinationals may be guilty of some wrongdoings from time to time, they are "essential for successful economic development." Liberals contend that multinationals often have too much power in relatively weak nations and that while their good aspects should be encouraged their power should be severely curtailed. The radical position, with which Magdoff associates himself, is that underdeveloped countries would be better off in the absence of multinationals. Going even further, Magdoff believes that "getting rid of the multinationals is a necessary but not sufficient condition" for third world countries to rid themselves of their poverty. He seeks a complete alteration of the power relations in these societies.

Magdoff challenges the conservatives' argument that multinationals provide third world countries with an opportunity to escape the "vicious circle of poverty" by bringing in foreign exchange and modern technology. He argues that multinationals contribute only a minor share of the money they invest, the bulk of it being raised in the host country and using up local savings. Furthermore, he says multinationals repatriate funds to the point where there is often a net capital outflow. On the matter of technological transfer, Magdoff claims that the multinational corporations are poorly equipped to do the job. The technical arts surrounding "sophisticated electronics or the mass production of autos and washing machines" are not what is needed in third world nations. What they require, according to Magdoff, are techniques to raise agricultural yields and products such as simple carts, wheelbarrows, bicycles, and pipes.

The fourth author in this volume, Dr. Gary C. Hufbauer, is Director of the U.S. Treasury's International Tax Staff. He explains the various principles of taxation and how they are related to multinational corporations. He focuses on the case of how U.S. multinationals have been treated under our tax laws, and he offers some suggestions for changing our international tax policy. Finally, he concerns himself with the question of protection of U.S. multinationals—i.e., How vigorously should the United States protect the foreign economic interests of multinational enterprises?

Dr. Hufbauer points to the foreign tax credit as the "keystone of U.S. taxation of American enterprise abroad." As it is administered, it gives U.S. multinationals a choice between being taxed the same at home as away, or being taxed at the same rate as any other firm located in the particular foreign country in which it operates. In cases where foreign tax rates are not too high and U.S. firms repatriate their foreign income, firms come close to being assured "capital-export neutrality." Alternatively, in those cases where U.S. firms choose not to repatriate funds, no tax is paid on foreign earnings and "capital-import neutrality" is achieved. Hufbauer believes, however, that it was the "functional taxation principle" rather than our trying to achieve neutrality of taxes that guided our decision to apply the foreign tax credit. He traces the foreign tax credit back to the 1950s and early 1960s when we wanted to encourage foreign investment in hopes that it would replace our massive program of foreign aid. Today, as exemplified by the Burke-Hartke bill that would repeal the foreign tax credit and only allow foreign taxes to be taken as a deduction, the mood has changed. While Hufbauer does not commit himself to the Burke-Hartke proposal, he advocates changes in our international tax policy that would discourage capital outflow. He reasons that, given our energy difficulties, substitutions of capital for energy will have to be made, and, also, that it would be desirable to have greater participation by local investors in the host countries.

Our fifth author, Professor Gerhard Rosegger, deals with the role of multinational corporations as agents of technological change. He suggests that extant international trade theory does an inadequate job of explaining international capital movements and that explanatory power can be greatly improved by introducing consideration of the role that multinationals play in diffusing technical innovations.

Rosegger explains that technological transfer is more than the mere transmission of information. The passage of technological information from one country to another qualifies as technological transfer, only when it is adopted on a significant scale by firms in the recipient country. Professor Rosegger points to several modes of technological transfer which are particularly suitable to multinationals' activities, such as the movement of technically competent people and the movement of capital equipment that embodied technology.

Utilizing a historical perspective, Rosegger divides the period since World War II into three phases: the years of U.S. government dominance, the period of heavy U.S. private capital flows abroad, and the "phase of convergence." Several of the other authors in this volume also recognize the first two of these phases, but the Rosegger suggestion that we are presently in a phase of technological convergence and that "the heyday of multinationals as agents in the rapid leveling of technology around the globe is already past" is a new and thought-provoking idea, which leads to the prediction of a slowing down of multinational expansion.

Our last author in this volume is Professor William G. Shepherd. While our previous five authors concentrated on analyzing the economic effects of U.S. multinationals operating in foreign countries, Shepherd examines "the scope for reversal"—the impact of foreign multinationals operating in the U.S. economy.

Professor Shepherd traces the set of international moves by U.S. firms since the beginning of this century and suggests that they may have run their course and that the balance may be shifting. He points to those U.S. industries which are characterized by high levels of monopoly control and offers the hypothesis that these "target industries" may be the "counterparts of the industries" which American firms have moved into abroad, "mopping up excess profits, energizing sluggish managements, increasing competition." He therefore suggests that foreign multinationals may be exactly what we've been looking for to combat our "monopoly problem," a problem that "natural erosion of market shares" and antitrust action have not been able to solve.

Having made the case for the benefits of foreign competition to America, Professor Shepherd explains that he really does not expect this competition to materialize on a grand scale. The reasons he provides include the following: (1) Foreign multinationals will lack the local banking connections which are required for successful entry; (2) they will not be able to overcome the "home court advantage" of U.S. firms, which can call on the official barriers of U.S. policies, processes, and agencies; (3) they will fear the retaliatory capabilities of large U.S. firms, and (4) many won't even be interested in competing against firms which they consider to be very well managed and tough. Nonetheless, Shepherd appeals to us not to undermine the little "corrective effect" that foreign multinationals operating in the United States have to offer.

Acknowledgments

I am grateful to the many individuals who helped me with the organization of this seminar and the preparation of this volume. Advice and assistance were provided by the members of the Department of Economics who served with me on the Lecture Series Committee, Alfred Ho and Louis Junker. Financial support, a necessary condition to carry out a project such as this, was arranged through the good offices of Dean Cornelius Loew, Associate Dean Tilman Cothran, and Professor

Raymond Zelder, Chairman of the Department of Economics. Four fine secretaries, Deborah Hochstetler, Em Hollingshead, Phyllis Kettlewell, and Cress Strand, did the typing, the retyping, and all the sundry chores associated with the preparation of the manuscript. The editorial work was skillfully performed by Mrs. Henrietta Slote and Ms. Alice Preketes of the Division of Research, Graduate School of Business Administration, University of Michigan.

I am very thankful to all of these people, but my greatest debt, of course, is to the authors whose papers appear in this volume. They visited Western Michigan University and delivered a version of the paper you are about to read for a price which I judge to be well below the market rate. Their reckless abandon of practicing what most economists preach can only be explained in terms of their devotion to education, their altruistic spirit, and their friendship.

W.S.

Kalamazoo, Mich.
May 1975

ABOUT THE CONTRIBUTORS

Authors

WILLIAM JAMES ADAMS *received his Bachelor's degree summa cum laude from Harvard University in 1969, and his Ph.D. in Economics from Harvard University in 1973. He taught economics during the 1973–74 academic year at Harvard and has recently joined the economics faculty at The University of Michigan. Professor Adams has written articles in the* Quarterly Journal of Economics *and the* Columbia Law Review *on the subjects of economic power, public policy, and European economic structure.*

GEORGE H. HILDEBRAND *is a well-known scholar and practitioner in the field of labor economics and industrial relations. He is Maxwell M. Upson Professor of Economics and Industrial Relations in the Department of Economics at Cornell University. The author of two books, one dealing with the Italian economy and the other examining manufacturing production functions in the United States, he has contributed essays and chapters to several other books and many articles to journals such as the* Labor Law Journal *and the* Harvard Business Review. *Professor Hildebrand is a past president of the Industrial Relations Research Association, a consultant to the Secretary of Labor, and an ad hoc and panel arbitrator, having heard over 500 cases during the past two decades. Before joining the faculty of Cornell University in 1960, Professor Hildebrand taught for a number of years at UCLA. From 1969 to 1971 he served as Deputy Undersecretary of Labor, U.S. Department of Labor.*

HARRY MAGDOFF *is co-editor of* Monthly Review. *He was in charge of statistical productivity studies for the WPA National Research Project on Re-employment Opportunities and Technological Development during the 1930s, and at that time designed the method of measuring production and productivity used to this day by the U.S. Department of Labor. During World War II he was chief of the Civilian Requirements Division of the National Defense Advisory Commission and later in charge of planning and controls in machinery industries for the War Production Board. Thereafter, he headed the Current Business Analysis Division of the U.S. Department of Commerce, and in that capacity was responsible for publishing the monthly* Survey of Current Business. *Magdoff's final years in government were spent as Special Assistant to the U.S. Secretary of Commerce, working first under Henry Wallace and later under Averell Harriman. Since that time he has been a financial consultant, stockbroker, insurance consultant, and publisher. He taught economics at the New School for Social Research, and has lectured at universities in the United States, Canada, and Europe. He is the author of* The Age of Imperialism, The Dynamics of U.S. Capitalism, *as well as of many articles and reviews.*

GARY C. HUFBAUER *is the Director of the International Tax Staff of the U.S. Treasury. Before joining the U.S. Treasury, he taught for about a decade at the University of New Mexico. During that time he participated with the Harvard Development Advisory Service in Pakistan for two years, served the Harvard Center for Population Studies, and was a Visiting Professor at Cambridge University and at the Stockholm School of Economics. Dr. Hubfbauer received an A.B. degree, magna cum laude, from Harvard College and a Ph.D. degree from King's College, Cambridge University. Among his many academic awards are: a Ford Foundation Faculty Fellowship, a National Science Foundation grant, and a Fulbright Research Scholarship. Dr. Hufbauer is the author of two books and a large number of articles, essays, and comments.*

GERHARD ROSEGGER *is Associate Professor and Chairman of the Department of Economics at Case Western Reserve University, where he also serves as a Senior Research Associate in the Research Program in Industrial Economics. Before coming to Case Western, he taught for five years at Rutgers University. Professor Rosegger is the author of many articles and chapters in books on the economics of the steel industry. He is currently completing a book,* Economic Effects of Technological Changes: The Case of U.S. Steel Manufacturing. *Dr. Rosegger is a referee for several economic journals as well as for the National Science Foundation. He is also a consultant to various business firms and trade associations.*

WILLIAM G. SHEPHERD *has taught economics at the University of Michigan for the past twelve years. Concurrently, he has served as a consultant to the Antitrust Division of the Department of Justice, the Senate Subcommittee on Antitrust and Monopoly, the President's Task Force on Communications, the Michigan Public Service Commission, and the U.S. Atomic Energy Commission, as well as to several city governments, foundations, and firms. During the academic year 1967–68, Dr. Shepherd was Special Economic Assistant to the Assistant Attorney General for Antitrust, U.S. Department of Justice. Professor Shepherd received the B.A. degree from Amherst College and the M.A. and Ph.D. degrees from Yale University. He spent one year as a Fulbright Fellow at the University of Glasgow. Dr. Shepherd is the author or editor of nine books. Among these are* Economic Performance under Public Ownership: British Fuel and Power, Market Power and Economic Welfare: An Introduction, The Treatment of Market Power, *and the 1975 revised edition of the late Clair Wilcox's* Public Policies toward Business.

Editor

WERNER SICHEL *is Professor of Economics at Western Michigan University. He received the B.S. at New York University, and the M.A. and Ph.D. in economics at Northwestern University. The author of a recent text,* Basic Economic Concepts, *Professor Sichel has also edited a number of books in the area of industrial organization:* Industrial Organization and Public Policy: Selected Readings, Antitrust Policy and Economic Welfare, *and* Public Utility Regulation: Change and Scope. *He is the author of a large number of articles, essays, and comments concerning antitrust policy, patent policy, conglomerate mergers and acquisitions, economic concentration, oligopoly theory, and business reciprocity. He has served as a consultant to several corporations, especially on patent policy. While Fulbright-Hays Senior Lecturer at the University of Belgrade, Professor Sichel pursued a research interest in the Yugoslavian economy. Currently he is President of the Economics Society of Michigan.*

MULTINATIONAL CORPORATIONS AND THE STATE OF COMPETITION: NEW REALITIES, OLD POLICY ISSUES

WILLIAM JAMES ADAMS

The international corporation can develop as a monopolist . . .or it can op-erate in the cosmopolitan interest to . . .enlarge competition. The choice is not solely up to the corporation; it depends largely on national policies . . . .

—Charles Kindleberger

Multinational corporations can be evaluated in many ways. The most prominent performance criteria observed in the popular literature range from stockholder profits to national employment levels, balance-of-payments positions, and foreign policies.[1] Less prevalent as a standard of performance is the impact multinationals have on the state of competition in source, host, and third countries.[2] The infrequency of research based on the competition benchmark is unfortunate, since the state of competition in turn determines the efficiency levels attained by national economies.

My purpose in this paper is to set forth the ways in which multinational corporations might influence the state of competition in national product markets. I begin with a demonstration that firms become multinational only when markets in both host and source countries are imperfect. I then suggest that multinationality is likely to reinforce rather than re-duce the initial imperfections, especially when it is accomplished via merger or joint venture. Finally, I appraise policy options, recommend-ing a ban on mergers and joint ventures involving one or more large firms.

Sources of Multinationality

In order to determine the impact of multinational corporations on the state of competition, we must understand why firms become multina-

1

tional in the first place.[3] To this end, let us explore a world characterized by two distinct national markets, A and B, and no commodity trade (because of, say, prohibitive transport costs). Let us suppose that initially firms produce, and hence sell, in either A or B (but not both) and that economic profits are being earned in A.

Conventional economic wisdom suggests that as long as market structure in A is competitive, new firms will enter and profits will vanish over time. Competitive market structure in A also implies that new entrants there will be domestic rather than foreign firms because foreign firms face certain disadvantages in penetrating even competitive markets: Their managers must often learn new languages and business customs; their communications lines may become overextended, making it difficult for key decision makers to keep abreast of developments in particular markets; and their stockholders must face the risk of discriminatory treatment by foreign governments, ranging from "buy domestic" campaigns to outright expropriation.

Given the natural disadvantages faced by firms which attempt to penetrate distant markets, multinationality is likely to occur only if foreign firms enjoy certain special advantages vis-à-vis their domestic counterparts. Stated somewhat differently, there must be barriers to the entry of domestic firms in A which do not apply to firms from B, if the latter are to become multinational in scope. What are these barriers which sometimes favor foreign firms?

Entry barriers may be lower for foreign than for domestic firms when the relevant market is characterized by product differentiation.[4] Firms already established in B may possess brands already desired in A, while new firms in A might have to spend heavily before achieving brand recognition anywhere. If advertisements used in B can be aired without change in A, moreover, firms already established in the former country can maintain their selling cost advantage over firms to be domiciled in the latter. The Coca Cola brand name, as well as the advertising campaigns of its owner, provide a perfect example of this kind of situation.[5]

Entry barriers may also be lower for foreign than for domestic firms when the relevant market is characterized by rapidly changing production technology.[6] The most advanced production processes are often first mastered in the most developed country. Firms located in that country might accordingly enjoy a production cost advantage in foreign countries with respect to their local potential competitors. The world-wide domination of IBM over computer technology affords a case in point.

Finally, entry barriers may be lower for foreign than for domestic firms when entry requires large sums of money. If foreign firms enjoy preferential access to investable funds, whether external or internal to the firm, they may displace local companies at the head of the entry queue. The absolute cost of oil refinery capacity constitutes one explanation, for example, of the foreign ownership of such capacity in many countries.

Thus, markets in the host country must be imperfect if foreign capital is to flow in. Host country market imperfections are not sufficient, however, to explain the rise of multinational corporations, since host country firms might seek to overcome their disadvantages by licensing the brand name, technology, or finance capital necessary to hurdle the entry barriers they face. Source country firms are reluctant to provide such licenses because they are unlikely to be able to specify requisite contracts with sufficient skill to capture all monopoly rents inherent in the foreign market.[7] If many source country firms enjoy the advantages of low entry barriers, however, competition among them should lead to licensing. Only if firms in the source country collectively boycott the licensing strategy will any of them be able to earn maximal monopoly profits abroad. Thus, market imperfections must characterize source as well as host countries if direct foreign investment is to occur.

Effects of Multinationality

From this cursory analysis, it is apparent that multinational corporations arise only in imperfect markets. Do they reduce or reinforce the imperfections which bring them into being? Analysts of industrial organization suggest that the extent of competition varies inversely with respect to two features of the market environment: the extent to which existing sellers (buyers) perceive and exploit their interdependence and hence behave collectively like a monopolist, and the extent to which existing sellers can partake of monopoly rents without provoking the birth of new firms.[8] The first condition is called mutual dependence recognized, while the second is termed barriers to new competition. Let us explore the effects of multinational corporations on these two market features in turn.

Mutual dependence recognized

The prevalence of mutual dependence recognized hinges on the profitability of collusion versus the profitability of independent behavior, as viewed by each seller (or buyer). Although a profit-maximizing monopolist necessarily earns more than does a competitive firm,[9] a participant in oligopolistic agreements enjoys no such guarantee. One reason is that collusive agreements are costly to devise and enforce. Another reason is that not all participants necessarily receive large shares of the spoils.

Neither the transactions costs nor the opportunity costs of agreements need be invariant with respect to changes in the market environment. The transactions costs of agreements depend heavily on the legal setting in which firms operate. If courts do not punish contracts in restraint of trade, then collusion can be practiced overtly, and hence agreements are cheaper to make. If courts actually *enforce* contracts restraining trade, then the public in effect subsidizes the cost of maintaining agreements, and hence collusion is cheaper still for the firm.

The opportunity cost of renouncing independent behavior is too difficult a concept to analyze completely here. For our purposes, it suffices to note that collusive agreements usually reward their participants in proportion to their actual share of the relevant market.[10] To the extent that current market shares are poor indicators of permanent or potential market shares,[11] at least some firms are likely to prefer independent to collusive conduct.

Before World War II, few national governments proscribed contracts restraining trade. As a result, collusion among firms took the form of national cartels regulating national markets, and international cartels regulating foreign trade.[12] Although different in several respects, most international cartels performed the same tasks:

1. Division of world markets
2. Establishment of export quotas
3. Prohibition of price-cutting in export markets

These cartels rarely worked to perfection, but they did permit greater recognition of mutual interdependence than would otherwise have occured.

After World War II, for a variety of reasons, many governments strengthened their competition policies by outlawing some forms of cartels. As a result, if collusion was to continue, it had to be tacit. The cost of tacit collusion depends critically on the number of firms involved in the scheme,[13] and the process of direct foreign investment is likely to alter that number, even though the direction of change is unclear. If direct investment takes the form of constructing new plants abroad, then multinationality increases the number of firms operating in the host country, without shrinking the number located in the source country. In this case, multinationality would appear to discourage the recognition of mutual interdependence.[14] If direct foreign investment takes the form of acquiring established firms abroad, then the number of firms in each country remains the same. The number of firms in the world as a whole, however, declines. Such decline facilitates collusion, as the following example suggests.

Suppose that the world is comprised of two national markets, A and B. Suppose, further, that each market is supplied by ten firms, only one of which owns plants in both countries. In this case, the double-market firm must come to terms with 18 competitors if it would coordinate the markets in which it operates. If each remaining firm in country A were to acquire a firm in country B, however, the initial firm would have to deal with only nine competitors. Fewness in a sense relevant to tacit coordination has increased, so that the state of competition has worsened. Notice that this result applies to the source as well as the host country.

Unfortunately, we possess little systematic evidence concerning the impact of direct investment on seller concentration. In two important respects, though, the actual pattern of multinationality conforms more closely to the perverse than to the benign. The first piece of evidence is that direct investment often proceeds via acquisition. In the automobile industry alone, American firms acquired such leading European companies as Opel, Vauxhall, Simca, and Rootes. In other industries international mergers are no less prevalent, as evidenced by the proposed absorptions (complete or partial) involving Aluminium Limited and National Distiller Chemical, British Petroleum and Standard Oil of Ohio, Shell and Sprague, Imperial Chemical Industries and Atlas Chemical, Gillette and Braun, Litton and Triumph-Adler, Schlitz and Labatt, and Continental Can and Thomassens Verblijfa.[15]

The second piece of evidence which renders the competitive impact of multinationality suspect is the parallel nature of most foreign investments. When one company from country A invests in country B, so do most of its leading competitors in A.[16] As firms producing in A are investing in B, firms producing in B are investing in A.[17] The conclusion to be drawn from this evidence is that much direct investment creates positions of parallel oligopoly and hence adversely affects the state of competition in source and host country alike.

The costs of schemes for tacit coordination depend on more than the number of participants. The less heterogeneous a given number of firms is in terms of national identity, for example, the easier tacit coordination will be for them. The reason is that business practices differ among countries, rendering tacit communication more difficult among strangers. In this sense, multinationality might generate competition in the host country even if it fails to increase the number of sellers there.

On the other hand, foreign investment might also permit recourse to institutional devices which facilitate coordination among firms.[18] One major institution of this kind is the joint venture. Because collusion can proceed overtly within joint ventures, the cost of conspiracy is reduced. Although sometimes declared illegal under American antitrust law,[19] joint ventures continue to flourish when their parents differ in nationality—the petroleum and chemical industries provide particularly good examples of ventures composed in this way—mainly because foreign governments favor transnational cooperation for political as well as economic reasons,[20] and American antitrust authorities, unwilling to jeopardize comity, may hesitate to prosecute even those cases over which they claim jurisdiction in principle.[21] Whatever the reason behind their durability, however, joint ventures afford an important instance of how multinationality can jeopardize the state of competition even if it augments the number of ostensible competitors.

The perverse competitive impact of joint ventures is not limited to the countries in which they reside. Judge Rifkind found in 1951 that the subsidiaries common to Imperial Chemical Industries and duPont de Nemours constituted focal points for trade restriction schemes involving the American market.[22] Earlier still, in the famous *Tobacco* case, a joint venture formed in the United Kingdom between American Tobacco and Imperial Tobacco, was found to affect American commerce adversely.[23] The joint ventures linking leading petroleum companies for the purpose of finding and producing crude oil illustrate the contemporary importance of this problem. These ventures not only facilitate formulation of restrictive agreements, but hinder subsequent cheating on them. The reason is that cheating in the form of price cutting is profitable only if accompanied by sales expansion. But sales expansion requires more crude oil, which is produced jointly with one's competitors. If price cutting occurs, therefore, the culprit can be identified rather easily: He is the one lifting more than his share of crude. Moreover, joint ventures facilitate development of crude oil pricing strategies which discourage lifting crude in excess of one's quota.[24]

Thus far, I have discussed only the transactions costs of collusion. I have argued that changes in antitrust policy after World War II prevented overt resurrection of the cartels which had been active between the world wars, and that direct foreign investment helped keep the costs of tacit collusion sufficiently low to insure its profitability. However, the shift from cartels to parallel foreign investment also reduced the opportunity cost of forgoing independent behavior. As a result, such a shift might have occurred even if world antitrust policy had remained the same as before the war.

One reason why the interwar cartels had heightened the opportunity cost of forgoing independent behavior was the inflexibility of their mechanism for distributing profits. The division of world markets, and hence profits, respected national boundaries. As a result, it was difficult to make small adjustments in the allocation of territory among national groups of producers. Yet such adjustments were continuously requested because of changes over time in both the bargaining strength of producers and the size of particular markets.[25]

Another reason why international cartels generally heighten the opportunity cost of forgoing independent behavior is that they subject producers to pressure from national governments preoccupied with balance-of-payments problems. The better an international cartel works, the more it suppresses commodity trade. Governments tend to ignore the relief from imports these schemes afford and to focus on their home firms' failure to export. They might threaten action against the domestic cartel unless exports are increased, rendering continued international agreements difficult for the national cartel to maintain.

Parallel foreign investments mitigate both these shortcomings of international cartels. Because each national producer group is located in each consuming market (via local subsidiaries), changes in both firm bargaining strengths and market growth characteristics can be taken in stride. Instead of deciding whether Argentina is to be an American or a German preserve, for example, the cartel can simply shift the split to 60-40 from 70-30. Moreover, because multinationals typically supply their foreign subsidiaries with components and technical services, they appear to contribute positively to source country balances of payments.[26]

I do not wish to imply that multinationality always shrinks the opportunity cost of renouncing independent behavior: Because multinationals maximize profits on a global level while single-country firms maximize profits on a national scale, the best strategy in any particular market may differ as between the two types of firms. As a result, a market populated exclusively with domestic sellers might experience more independent rivalry if penetrated by a multinational than if entered by another domestic enterprise.[27] If the reason for multinational entry is an advantage in product differentiation, however, the independent behavior will seldom involve price competition. Moreover, the greater the extent of *mutual* interpenetration, the less likely is independent behavior, since aggression by a firm abroad might provoke retaliation against it at home.[28]

We possess only fragmentary knowledge concerning the extent to which mutual interdependence is recognized across countries. For our purposes, however, it suffices to show that direct foreign investment enhances international collusion more than does commodity trade as regulated by cartels. Few would deny the empirical accuracy of such a proposition.[29]

Barriers to new competition

I suggested earlier that multinationality occurs only when the barriers to new competition faced by domestic potential entrants exceed those faced by their foreign counterparts. It might seem, therefore, that allowance of direct foreign investment swells the pool of potential entrants in each national market and lowers the maximum rate of return that established firms can earn without provoking entry. Despite this felicitous result, multinationality might also serve to elevate the barriers to new competition. Three ways in which this can occur bear discussion.

First, the height of barriers to new competition depends on the profits entrants expect to earn once they are established, as well as on the costs they incur to commence operations. The greater the established firms' capabilities for retaliation against entrant firms, the higher the barriers to new competition. Now multinationals find it easier to retaliate against domestic potential entrants than do their single market colleagues. As long as the multinationals operate in several markets, and as long as they earn satisfactory profits elsewhere, they hardly feel the impact of temporarily low profits in any particular market. Potential entrants know this and might believe they would face damaging predation upon establishment. This prospect discourages entry.

There is some disagreement in the economics literature concerning the logic behind this argument. Specifically, there is some doubt that a profit-maximizing multinational would price below cost in particular markets even if it earned good profits in others. Complete resolution of the debate is impossible here, but two remarks may help to clarify the issues. In the first place, pricing below (marginal) cost is not the relevant criterion for determining the extent of predatory activity. Profits need not vanish to ensure that entry will not occur.[30] In the second place, the low profits to be earned by the multinational can be considered an *investment* in keeping entry barriers high. Low profits are endured in the short run in the expectation of high monopoly returns in the long run.

Many students of the multinational have tried to determine whether foreign investors in fact use high profits earned in some markets to offset low profits earned in other markets. Barnet and Mueller report that such cross-subsidization is prevalent in multinational enterprises,[31] but not all observers agree. Since foreign subsidiaries often publish their own financial accounts, this empirical issue would appear relatively easy to resolve. If cross-subsidization does in fact occur, one would expect to observe the following financial patterns: high variance in profitability across subsidiaries of a given firm at any point in time; high variance over time in the profitability of a given subsidiary; and little positive correlation between a given subsidiary's profit rank within the firm in one period and the same subsidiary's profit rank in another period.[32]

Until we have the results of such empirical tests, it is useful to note that multiregional firms within the United States, which are in the abstract, economic sense analytically equivalent to multinational firms, are known to practice cross-subsidization of the sort described here. For example, baking companies engaged in two forms of price discrimination in their bid to exterminate local market competitors. The first, called route price discrimination, occurred when a lower price was charged far away from a plant than was charged close by, despite the existence of transport costs. The second, called plant price discrimination, occurred when lower prices were charged at some plants than at others, even though costs were identical at the two production sites. The low prices did not last, of course. Once local competitors withdrew from the market, prices were set above competitive levels. Similar pricing histories are associated with the brewing, gasoline distribution, and grocery industries.[33]

2. The second perverse impact of multinationals on the barriers to entry occurs when foreign investments are consumated via merger. If a leading firm in country A acquires a leading firm in country B, the latter is unlikely to establish its own plants in A. It may even discontinue exports to A. In entry barrier terminology, foreign acquisitions entail removal of existing foreign firms from the queue of potential entrants into the home market. As a result, the barriers to new competition in the source country rise. To the extent that the acquiring firm is now unlikely to build its own plants abroad, barriers rise in the host country as well.

An excellent example of this process involves the attempt by Schlitz to acquire the Canadian brewer Labatt.[34] Both firms sold beer in the western United States; Labatt, through a subsidiary, controlled 13 percent of the market, while Schlitz controlled 10 percent. In finding the merger illegal, the Supreme Court referred not simply to the suppression of this actual competition, but to the elimination of potential competition from Labatt in the United States considered as a whole. The potential competition issue also played a role in the *Monsanto, Aluminium, Ltd., Standard* (Ohio), and *Imperial Chemical Industries* cases cited earlier.[35]

We have less evidence concerning the effect of international acquisitions on the suppression of commodity trade, but it seems hardly fortuitous that Simca stopped exporting to the United States shortly after its acquisition by Chrysler while other French automobile manufacturers continued to sell in the American market.

3. The last effect of multinational corporations on the height of barriers to new competition is more subtle than the other two. It consists of using the political leverage such corporations have to exclude potential competitors. In the 1920s, for example, two American sisal dealers established a buying outlet in Mexico. Through a variety of political ploys, they secured discriminatory legislation against all actual and potential competitors, to be enforced by both the national and the provincial governments.[36]

Even in developed economies, public policies toward business often raise rather than lower barriers to entry.[37] By permitting its manufacturers to form export cartels under the Webb-Pomerene Act, the American government hoped to help them overcome the allegedly evil machinations of international cartels when attempting to penetrate foreign markets. Instead, Webb associations discouraged foreign distributors from handling the merchandise of rival American firms, and the export business of such rivals was accepted only at discriminatory fees. As a result, barriers to competition rose in the foreign commerce of the United States.[38] I suspect that current efforts by European governments to create domestic firms "of world scale" will result in similar diminutions of competition.

The effects of multinationals on public policy are extremely dangerous because they cannot be detected easily. When American dairy farmers seek the favors governments can bestow, they hire lobbyists as well as engage (and get caught) in illegal activities. When major American manufacturing companies seek the same favors, no such conduct is required.[39] Explicit or implicit threats to move abroad are sufficient to bring labor, suppliers, and dealers to entreat government on their behalf. By their very actions in the international arena, multinationals tell governments what they wish to be done. As a result, to chart political influence in terms of overt lobbying practices is to underestimate rather seriously the role of the multinational corporation.

Policy Options

How should national governments treat direct foreign investment if they wish to improve the state of competition in their economies? At the very least, they should require multinationals to divulge certain data concerning their operations. The need for such a requirement stems from the inability to resolve the impact of multinationals on competition without recourse to empirical information. Particularly useful would be a requirement that each firm above some threshold size report its sales, employment, assets, and costs and place such information in matrix form, with countries of the world represented as one dimension and four-digit SIC industries represented as the other.

In addition to requiring more information, governments should end artificial inducements to multinationality, such as tariffs, tax loopholes, and merger subsidies. The most important single step of this kind, after freedom of commodity trade, would be to end the allowance of foreign tax credits against domestic tax liability. Public insurance of private risks abroad, as represented by OPIC in the United States, should also be pruned substantially.

These two steps might remove whitecaps from the waves of foreign investment, but they are by themselves unlikely to restore competition in world markets. As a result, I believe governments should go one step further and prohibit any leading firm from participating in an international merger or joint venture. If my analysis of the effects of multinationals on competition is sound, then such a law should eliminate precisely those types of foreign investment which harm competition, without affecting those types which promote it. If still more potent policies are indicated, then Horst's proposal to trim leading firms of existing foreign subsidiaries deserves serious consideration.[40]

A ban on international mergers and joint ventures is not as impractical as it sounds. From a procedural standpoint, close international cooperation among antitrust authorities may not be required. American courts already claim jurisdiction over both acts committed and firms domiciled abroad, if either element contributes to conspiracies in restraint of American commerce.[41] Such jurisdiction is claimed even when foreign governments are involved in the restrictive scheme.[42] In similar, if less pervasive, fashion the European Court of Justice has also claimed jurisdiction over firms not domiciled in the European Communities so long as Community trade is affected.[43] There is even evidence to suggest that governments considered hostile to direct investment are upset more by merger than by creation of new plants.[44] As long as the jurisdictional options of these judicial systems are exercised, virtually no international merger or joint venture need escape prosecution. Existing governments can achieve competition almost unilaterally, should they so desire.[45]

From a substantive standpoint, there is also ample precedent for the kinds of prohibitions advocated here. In the United States, several international mergers have been prevented on the basis of diminished actual or potential competition.[46] Many joint ventures have also been prevented on the same grounds.[47] The European Court of Justice has recently ruled that mergers can be prohibited under the Treaty of Rome, and the European Commission (if not the Court) was prepared to prevent an international merger which involved suppression of potential competition.[48]

If multinational corporations appear to be new forms on the industrial landscape, the policy problems they generate have nevertheless faced society for some time. Today's multinationals, like yesterday's cartels and last week's multiregionals, arise only in imperfect markets.[49] Although in principle these types of enterprise can reinforce or reduce the imperfections which brought them to life, we should have learned by now that the perverse effect is likely to dominate as long as a firm arises from major merger or joint venture. Yet, we have not proscribed such activities per se. Given the advanced state of antitrust policy in this area, the time to do so is now.

Notes

The strong influence of Richard Caves and Thomas Horst on this paper will be apparent to even casual students of multinational corporations.

1. For introductions to the subject of multinational corporations at various levels of technical sophistication, see Barnet and Mueller (1974), Caves (1971), Horst (1972), Kindleberger (1970), and Vernon (1971).

2. Although see Caves (1974) and Horst (1975).

3. For my purposes, any firm possessing tangible fixed assets in more than one country is multinational in scope. Therefore, there is a one-to-one correspondence between multinational enterprise and direct foreign investment. I shall use the two terms interchangeably.

4. See Caves (1971).

5. The product differentiation advantage of multinational companies is not always as plausible empirically as it might seem to be *a priori*. If foreign investment proceeds via merger, then the advantage of the multinational cannot be ascribed to its existing brands. And if the advertisements associated with any particular brand differ depending on where they are presented, then the argument of scale economies in advertising falls through as well. My own impressions of American advertising on Canadian television (Windsor, Ontario) suggest that the sales pitch for a given product differs markedly in the two countries. What is called a selling *cost* advantage, therefore, may be a selling *funds* advantage.

6. See Vernon (1966).

7. Consider the Coca Cola case. Should the American corporation require that the distinctive Coca Cola script and bottles be used? that the famous syrup have the same sugar content as in the United States? that the advertising theme include "things go better with Coke" or "Coke is the real thing"? And under what circumstances should the contract prescribe *changes* in strategy to enhance profits?

8. See Bain (1968).

9. Assuming the market demand curve is downward sloping.

10. See Stocking and Watkins (1946).

11. The new firm usually enters at a scale below that which it hopes to attain relative to its competitors. And the firm primarily resident in other markets might wield more power in this market than its market share indicates. I pass over the special cases, like that involving General Motors, in which a firm does not seek maximal market share because of potential antitrust prosecution.

12. See Stocking and Watkins (1946).

13. See Stigler (1968), chap. 5.

14. For reasons other than its impact on fewness, however, a multinational might still have a perverse influence on mutual dependence recognized.

15. See, respectively, *U.S.* v. *Aluminium Ltd.,* 268 F.Supp. 758 (D.N.J. 1966); *U.S.* v. *Standard Oil* (Ohio), 1970 Trade Cases Para. 72,988 (consent decree); In re: Imperial Chemical Industries, 1972 Federal Trade Commission (consent decree); *U.S.* v. *Gillette,* Civil Action 68-141-W, Filed February 14, 1968, D. Mass.; In re: Litton Industries, Federal Trade Commission Docket 8778, Apr. 10, 1969; *U.S.* v. *Schlitz,* 253 F.Supp. 129 (D.Cal. 1966); and *Europemballage* v. *E.C. Commission,* 2 Com.Mkt.Rep. Para. 8171 (Court of Justice, Feb. 21, 1973).

16. See Horst (1974) and Knickerbocker (1973).

17. See Kindleberger (1970), pp. 32–33.

18. The very choice of direct investment over exports as the mechanism for servicing a foreign market makes it easier to keep abreast of foreign market developments, which include foreign collusion schemes.

19. See *U.S.* v. *American Tobacco Co.,* 221 U.S. 106 (1911); *U.S.* v. *United States Alkali Export Assoc.,* 86 F. Supp. 59 (S.D.N.Y. 1949); and *U.S.* v. *Imperial Chemical Industries,* 100 F.Supp. 504 (S.D.N.Y. 1951).

20. See the memorandum to the governments of member states sent by the Commission of the European Economic Community in 1965 urging favorable treatment of transnational mergers within the Common Market (1965 Com.Mkt.Rep. Para. 9481).

21. Perhaps that is why the trial judge in the *Cellophane* case found that it is "lawful for an American and a French concern who are not competitors to combine their resources in a joint venture absent an overriding unlawful purpose." *U.S.* v. *E.I. duPont de Nemours,* 118 F.Supp. 41, 220 (D.Del. 1955).

22. *U.S.* v. *Imperial Chemical Industries.*

23. *U.S.* v. *American Tobacco Co.*

24. See the Subcommittee on Multinational Corporations of the Senate Foreign Relations Committee (1974), Part 7.

25. See Stocking and Watkins (1946).

26. See the Senate Finance Committee (1973), for calculations to the effect that U.S. multinationals contribute positively to the American balance of payments.

27. See Caves (1974).

28. See Knickerbocker (1973).

29. See Caves (1974) for a more complete discussion of this point.

30. A similar position is taken in Yamey (1972). The critical profit level at which entry begins to occur can be related to Bain's concept of a "limit" price. See Bain (1956) and Caves and Porter (1975).

31. See Barnet and Mueller (1974).

32. This research design is not entirely free of complications. Depending on how national

governments set profits tax and tariff rates, multinationals might under- or over-state profits in the financial accounts of their subsidiaries. As long as enough subsidiaries are studied over time, however, and as long as parents from enough countries are included in the sample, the problems associated with tax loopholes can be neutralized.

33. See Blair (1972).

34. *U.S.* v. *Schlitz,* 253 F.Supp. 129 (D.Cal. 1966).

35. See note 15.

36. See *U.S.* v. *Sisal Sales Corp.,* 274 U.S. 286 (1927).

37. See Adams (1955).

38. See *U.S.* v. *United States Alkali Export Assoc.,* and *U.S.* v. *Minnesota Mining and Manufacturing Co.,* 92 F.Supp. 947 (D. Mass. 1950). See also Fugate (1973), p. 353.

39. Which is not to say that it is not used. Witness the successful attempts of American petroleum companies to induce the American government to use its influence in Libya to achieve an increase in crude oil prices, and to limit the number of American firms with concessions throughout the Middle East. Witness also the hundreds of thousands of dollars the former head of United Brands paid to Central American and European governments as bribes for preferential treatment of his company's goods, before he leaped from the forty-fourth floor of a Manhattan skyscraper.

40. See Horst (1975).

41. The evolution of judicial thinking on these matters is clear. See *American Banana Co.* v. *United Fruit Co.,* 213 U.S. 347 (1909); *U.S.* v. *American Tobacco Co.,* 221 U.S. 106 (1911); and *U.S.* v. *Sisal Sales Corp.,* 274 U.S. 286 (1927).

42. See *U.S.* v. *Sisal Sales Corp.,* 274 U.S. 286 (1927); and *Continental Ore Co.* v. *Union Carbide and Carbon Corp.,* 370 U.S. 690 (1962).

43. *Imperial Chemical Industries* v. *E.C. Commission,* 2 Com.Mkt.Rep. Para. 8161 (Ct. of Justice 1972).

44. For example, Pichard du Page and Turot (1970), p. 46, report that "French authorities insist on distinguishing between foreign investments which involve mere acquisition of existing French firms, and investments which entail creation of new plants equipped with advanced technology." (My translation.)

45. I urge the unilateral approach on grounds of pragmatic feasibility alone. International cooperation is certainly the preferred route as long as it is a genuine option.

46. For example, *U.S.* v. *Schlitz,* 253 F.Supp. 129 (D. Cal. 1966).

47. See *U.S.* v. *Penn-Olin Chemical Co.,* 378 U.S. 158 (1964); and, in the international sphere, *U.S.* v. *Monsanto,* 1967 Trade Cases Para. 72,001 (D.Pa. 1967) (consent decree).

48. *Europemballage* v. *E.C. Commission,* 2 Com.Mkt.Rep. Para. 8171.

49. Barnet and Mueller (1974) draw the analogy between multinationals and conglomerates. I believe the analogy between multinationals and multiregionals is closer.

References

Adams, Walter, and Horace Gray. *Monopoly in America*. New York: Macmillan, 1955.

Bain, Joe S. *Barriers to New Competition*. Cambridge, Mass.: Harvard University Press, 1956.

___. *Industrial Organization*. 2d ed. New York: Wiley & Sons, 1968.

Barnet, Richard I., and Ronald E. Mueller. *Global Reach: The Power of the Multinational Corporations*. New York: Simon and Schuster, 1974.

Blair, John M. *Economic Concentration*. New York: Harcourt Brace Jovanovich, 1972.

Caves, Richard E. "International Corporations: The Industrial Economics of Foreign Investment." *Economica* 38 (Feb. 1971): 1–27.

___. "International Trade, International Investment, and Imperfect Markets." Special Papers in International Economics. No. 10. Princeton University, Nov. 1974.

___. and Michael E. Porter. "From Entry Barriers to Mobility Barriers: Conjectural Decisions and Contrived Deterrence to New Competition." Harvard Institute of Economic Research, Discussion Paper No. 401, Feb. 1975.

Fugate, Wilbur L. *Foreign Commerce and the Antitrust Laws*. 2d ed. Boston, Mass.: Little, Brown, 1973.

Horst, Thomas. "American Investments Abroad and Domestic Market Power." Unpublished manuscript, The Brookings Institution, 1975.

___. *At Home Abroad: A Study of the Domestic and Foreign Operations of the American Food-Processing Industry*. Cambridge, Mass.: Ballinger, 1974.

___. "Firm and Industry Determinants of the Decision to Invest Abroad: An Empirical Study." *Review of Economics and Statistics* 54 (Aug. 1972) 258–66.

Kindleberger, Charles (ed.). *The International Corporation*. Cambridge, Mass.: MIT Press, 1970.

Knickerbocker, Frederick T. *Oligopolistic Reaction and Multinational Enterprise*. Boston, Mass.: Harvard Graduate School of Business Administration, 1973.

Pichard du Page, Roger, and Paul Turot. *Les Sociétés internationales*. Paris, France: La Documentation Française, 1970.

Stigler, George J. *The Organization of Industry*. Homewood, Ill.: Irwin, 1968.

Stocking, George W., and Myron W. Watkins. *Cartels in Action*. New York: Twentieth Century Fund, 1946.

U.S. Senate, Committee on Finance, Subcommittee on International Trade. *The Multinational Corporation and the World Economy*. Washington, D.C.: Government Printing Office, 1973.

____. Committee on Foreign Relations, Subcommittee on Multinational Corporations. *Hearings on Multinational Petroleum Companies and Foreign Policy*, Part 7. Washington, D.C.: Government Printing Office, 1974.

Vernon, Raymond. "International Investment and International Trade in the Product Cycle." *Quarterly Journal of Economics* 80 (May 1966): 190–207.

____. *Sovereignty at Bay*. New York: Basic Books, 1971.

Yamey, Basil S. "Predatory Price Cutting." *Journal of Law and Economics* 40 (April 1972): 129–42.

MULTINATIONAL CORPORATIONS: THEIR GENERAL SIGNIFICANCE AND THEIR RELATION TO HOME EMPLOYMENT

GEORGE H. HILDEBRAND

Sequence of development

The multinational corporation is an enterprise with a central head-quarters and a span of administrative control that encompasses branch plants or subsidiaries in other countries. In the long history of the modern Western world, companies of this sort first made their appearance in trade, banking, and shipping. In fact firms survive in the Far East that have this kind of origin. The basic pattern was set long before, with firms—some of them going back to the early seventeenth century—which typically emerged as mercantilistic trading monopolies in various places, for examples, the Dutch East India Company, the British East India Company, or more recently, the Congo Company (1885).

For purposes of the present discussion, we should concentrate on the privately owned and controlled multinational corporation. This is not to deny the existence of similar institutions which are in fact government enterprises or public corporations, such as the Russian group that built the Orissa steel mill in India, or the Chinese group that is just completing the Tanzam railway in Zambia and Tanzania. These interesting ventures are not, however, guided by profit-maximizing intent; they are not privately owned; and they are not risk-bearing, market-oriented enterprises. Moreover, for more or less ideological reasons they have not come under systematic attack, while the private multinational corporations have become the chosen targets of various socialist movements and international agencies of the United Nations.

It is a peculiarity of these private concerns that by their long administrative reach they can influence labor relations, employment, working conditions, and wages in countries other than the one in which their cen-

17

tral control exists. Collaterally, it should be noted that to a degree, although not completely, these firms provide a substitute for the older form of international trade in which a company in Country A produces goods and then exports them through second and third parties for eventual sale in Country B. The latter represents the classical form of international trade. The multinational concern eliminates the intermediary, and the company itself handles the movement, either as exports from Country A or indeed as imports into A from B, with the whole process under the control of the same administrative organization. Moreover, these concerns also control international capital flows. Traditionally, these flows have involved concerns in a given country which go abroad to a money market center, such as London or New York, to obtain financing for large capital projects—the building of railroads, or the development of mines, factories, or other facilities. This kind of transaction involves a complicated relationship that extends from ultimate investors through intermediary investment bankers to the company ultimately issuing the securities. Much of the American railroad system in the 19th century was built in this fashion. In the case of the multinational today, however, the situation is one in which enterprise can mobilize its own capital at the center, shift it around under its own control at all times, and undertake substantial investments without direct entry into the capital market of any country.

Returning for a moment to the late sixteenth and early seventeenth centuries, the international firms at that time essentially were companies chartered to engage in trade. Here the British East India Company is the great example. However, it should be pointed out that the company soon discovered that if it were to engage successfully in trade it would literally have to erect an administrative state, and to raise and supply troops to preserve order. By the nineteenth century the pattern had changed to some extent: the object of going abroad had now become mainly that of mining and refining, and still later of extracting petroleum. Here the careers of Cecil Rhodes and his colleagues are of great interest, initially for their development of the diamond minds at Kimberley in the 1870s, and then in the Rand gold mines after 1886. Although these ventures were private in nature, they were, from their inception, intimately involved in politics, including international politics. By contrast, the parallel Congo Company, also private in a technical sense, happened to be owned by the King of the Belgians, who had made himself the absolute ruler of the Congo, establishing thereby a strange union of private enterprise with the state.

After World War I the multinational company began to appear not only in mining and resource extraction, but in public utilities and manufacturing also. One can therefore say with some safety that the sequence has run from trade through extractive industries to public utilities and ultimately into manufacturing, where the multinational now plays its largest role. One can also say that the multinationals gained their greatest strength in the period after the Second World War, where, for certain reasons, it became possible for these companies to expand rapidly, while the incentive to do so was greatly strengthened by various facets of international trade and currency policies. In consequence a flood of these new ventures have emerged, originating in countries as diverse as the United States, West Germany, the United Kingdom, Holland, France, Italy, and Japan. Of the entire group, the United States clearly has been the leader.

In seeking to account for the phenomenon, one notes that a chief facilitating factor has been great developments in modern communications and air transport, which have allowed the span of control to be extended without loss of effective managerial coordination. This has made it possible to make decisions from a distance on the basis of up-to-date information which is quickly and continuously available, to send people out to distant points and to bring other people in, and to do all this without great loss of time.

It would be a mistake to assume that the sole role for the United States in this process is to serve as a donor for private capital to be used abroad. On the contrary, we are also a host country for foreign private capital, now to the extent of over $17 billion. (As one small illustration, the Japanese have just completed a small steel mill in Auburn, New York.)

On the other side of the ledger, the United States has now expended approximately $95 billion in direct private investments abroad. It is this huge outflow of American capital which has done the most to make the multinational corporation so prominent a political issue, both here and abroad. Significantly, too, the movement began to gather speed in 1965—at the same time that inflation started to accelerate here—in a context in which, until 1973, the dollar was kept in fixed parity with both gold and the exchange rates of the other countries in the free world. I am suggesting that as the dollar progressively became over-valued under the one-sided Bretton Woods system, it became more and more difficult for the United States to export goods and services, and more and more attractive for American companies to export dollars to buy foreign subsidiaries and to build foreign plants. This is not the whole story, of course, but it is a very important part of the story.

Distribution of investment

To grasp the impact of these capital exports on home employment in the United States, it is helpful to look at the geographic pattern of these investments as well as their distribution among the major branches of economic activity. Of the cumulative total of $94 billion in direct foreign investments by American business as of 1971, the geographic distribution is as follows: 28 percent in Canada, 32 percent in Europe and the United Kingdom, 5.7 percent in Australia, New Zealand, and South Africa, and 2.1 percent in Japan. The remaining 32 percent is scattered over the rest of the world, mainly in Central and Northern Africa, Latin America, and the Middle East, with a figure for the Middle East which, of course, reflects the enormous oil complex in that part of the world. Also worthy of notice is Canada's very high place in the total picture. For good or ill, it illustrates the close interdependence of Canada and the United States. By contrast, there is the very low figure for Japan, despite its great industrial importance. This reflects the longstanding Japanese mercantilist policy of denying significant amounts of foreign capital admission into the country. Indeed, when it is allowed to enter, the outside interest must accept minority status.

Looking at the distribution in its historical dimension, we find that between 1960 and 1971 $32 billion of direct foreign investment for private account was made, increasing the cumulative total by 50 percent in the period. After 1964 the bulk of this investment was distributed quite closely in the fashion indicated for the terminal year 1971. In other words, Canada and Europe were dominant; the rest of the world was third; Australia and its group were next, and Japan ended up at the bottom.

Next, consider the distribution of these direct foreign investments by major function. Here the numbers are relatively crude, but still they are indicative. As of 1971, manufacturing accounted for $35.5 billion of the cumulative total, or 41 percent. By contrast, 7.8 percent was accounted for mining and smelting—activities that turn up to some extent in Canada but appear mainly in Africa, Australia and New Zealand, and Latin America. Petroleum accounted for 28.3 percent. Thus, raw materials extraction in some form absorbed over one-third of the cumulative total of direct foreign investment by the United States. This point is worthy of strong emphasis because it tells us that a huge chunk of this overseas investment by private companies has gone into raw materials production rather than into duplicate plant facilities and manufacturing, although at the same time, 41 percent in manufacturing is clearly not to be overlooked. It is also worthy of note that the manufacturing component grew a little faster during the preceding decade than did the rest of these sectors.

Summing up, then, we find that manufacturing is very important, that Western Europe and Canada are very significant host areas for American investment, that the extraction of raw materials is also very important, and that such extractive activities tend to be in areas other than Western Europe.

Accordingly, we reach at last the question: What significance do these data hold for home employment and unemployment in the United States?

Impact on Employment at Home

The first fact to be noted is that while the South East Asian industrial group—Taiwan, Hong Kong, Singapore, and, stretching geography a little, South Korea—does not receive large sums in total direct foreign investments, it does involve manufacturing activities which are closely competitive with similar activities in the continental United States. All of these countries are very prominent in light manufacturing and assembly of electronic goods, in apparel, and other industries of this kind. Typically these industries involve labor-intensive production, simple types of mechanization, and, accordingly, a high sensitivity to wage costs. As a result, the availability of qualified cheap labor can make a real difference in attracting and holding this type of business. The two great cases in this field are Taiwan and Hong Kong. Within the past decade Taiwan has captured a big chunk of the light fabricating and assembly business in television sets, radio sets, and other electronic goods, precisely because its wages are low, there are no unions, and the work force is still strongly influenced by the Chinese variant of the work ethic. The people of Taiwan are highly productive, hard workers, and they are easy to train and quick to learn. Once American manufacturers found themselves badly squeezed at home by the growing competition of Japanese substitutes, they found a shift of production to Taiwan to be both technically feasible and profitable. In fact, this shift was the price of survival. Indeed, there is a bit of irony in this story, for now the Japanese manufacturers in these fields are undertaking the same migration to escape high production costs at home.

Consider, next, overseas private American investments in mining and petroleum, which, you will recall, account for 36 percent of the total. In the main, these activities are not closely competitive with domestic production. For example, the United States has an import surplus in petroleum. That is to say, we take in more petroleum from abroad than we export, with most of these imports coming from Venezuela and some from the Middle East. When we supplement domestic production with additional output from foreign sources, we do not lose jobs thereby, although it could be argued that if we shut off these foreign sources completely we would then be compelled to develop domestic replacements at much higher costs—replacements that are not being developed now simply because they are unprofitable. In this special sense, then, a few potential jobs are lost in the domestic extraction and refining of petroleum, but as this industry is highly capital intensive, the number of jobs cannot be of much significance.

Another illustration can be drawn from copper mining. The United States has an import surplus of copper, drawn principally from South America, while Western Europe gets its copper primarily from South Africa and partly from Chile. As with petroleum, it would make no sense to argue that if we buy some copper from Chile we are displacing American copper miners from their jobs, because we start with an import surplus and the only jobs involved would be the potential ones that *might* be created if we instituted a program of systematic autarky.

In passing, it is appropriate to ask why American firms go abroad to produce copper or petroleum when undoubtedly they could expand production here at home. The simple answer is that it is profitable to go abroad because richer deposits are found there. In other words, production costs are lower, so it pays to make these investments. It should also be pointed out that the corporations involved have long since acquired the managerial skills and technical capacity to develop foreign production, and that most of this foreign production in the case of both copper and petroleum is sold in Europe, not in the United States. The object is not to deprive American workers of jobs, but to make overseas investments which are profitable in themselves. As a result, Europe can have low-cost raw materials imports, South Africa and the Middle East can have high-wage jobs for their workers and export earnings for their international accounts, and American investors can obtain competitive rates of return on their money. Behind the whole complicated business is the fact that nature did not distribute raw material deposits evenly over the earth. It is this central fact, not preservation of the rate-of-surplus value, which is the reason capital is exported in the extractive industries.

But what about capital export for overseas manufacturing? Here is where American labor unions are most concerned; it is this kind of investment that they condemn as "run-away shops in search of cheap labor." The problem any union must always overcome is incomplete control of the market for the services of their members in any given industry. If the organization does not control all of the plants producing for the same product market, then its strikes will be ineffective, its power to raise wages and to improve conditions will be crippled, and it will be under constant threat from the nonunion competitors. As John R. Commons, a great economist at the University of Wisconsin, pointed out back in 1908 in his famous essay on the history of the American shoemakers, unions that are unable to control all of the substitute sources of supply cannot negotiate effectively.

Now it would be a mistake to assume that all direct American foreign investment in manufacturing has the purpose of creating substitute plants beyond the control of domestic unions. Concerns may go abroad to manufacture for reasons that have nothing to do with escaping standards set in American collective bargaining. In the first place, the output to be produced abroad may be very different from what is manufactured here and in fact may not even be available for export from the United States. Finished manufacturing goods tend to be highly differentiated, whereas inputs such as copper or steel are much more homogeneous.

But beyond this, an American firm can go abroad simply because that is the only way it can avoid foreign trade barriers which deny it the opportunity to export directly from the United States. The Common Market countries are a notorious case in point. Often U.S. firms have better technology and better management than their foreign competitors, and they may also have access to economies of scale, all of which work together to make it profitable for them to enter foreign markets through the medium of direct investments in such countries. In this case there is no loss of domestic (U.S.) jobs; the barriers to American exports have foreclosed production for such purposes in the first place. In some instances, for example automobiles, a related factor may well be that American producers have faced short-run saturation in domestic demand, and thus find it profitable to invest in plants in countries where the demand for motor cars is rapidly expanding with rising incomes.

Still another motive leading to direct investment abroad involves the profits of integration. Briefly, a concern may wish to gain control of raw material sources abroad, either to assure a cheap and effective source for its domestic production, or to preempt access by competitors. Preemption of foreign sources of raw materials was a dramatic factor in borax and borates at the close of the nineteenth century and in bauxite for aluminum somewhat later. Neither instance involved a curtailment of home employment, although the objective was to get a better home price for the final product. In other instances, however, vertical integration to assure supplies of raw materials has been motivated not by monopoly considerations but simply because richer deposits abroad provided opportunity for profitable investments. This essentially is the story in copper and petroleum, or iron ore in Australia. On the other hand, when companies go abroad to achieve horizontal integration, that is to say, to bring their competitors under one roof, injury can occur to all consumer interest. But again, the problem here is not one of denying jobs to American workers. Nor, in my opinion, is the case at all common when the whole array of direct foreign investment by American firms is considered.

What I am really contending in a rather clandestine way is that trade is to the benefit of the traders, and that multinational corporations have been a powerful encouragement for increased international trade. Fringe cases of monopoly here and there should not obscure the very positive world-wide benefits involved. Indeed, multinational firms promote an optimal use of capital around the world, and they also benefit the consumers of the world.

However, when we get into the question of impact on domestic workers, the story grows somewhat more complex. I have suggested that the bulk of direct investments overseas can not be interpreted as involving export of American jobs. But I also contend that the international economic policy of the United States since 1945 has indeed had injurious effects on home employment. This matter results far more from official policy than from actions of the multinational corporations themselves.

Since World War II the United States has been experiencing a prolonged inflationary boom that only now seems to be coming to an end. These years have been marked by rising trends in total employment, in real wages, and in national output—interrupted only by brief and shallow recessions. Although the general rate of unemployment has exceeded 4 percent throughout most of these years, on the whole the reasons for this rather high rate are not found in any deficiency of total demand for goods and services.

The financial conditions associated with this world-wide boom are important to home employment. They derive in part from the system of fixed parities of exchange established under the Bretton Woods system in 1944 and in part from the almost endless chain of deficits in our international balance of payments extending back to 1950. Under the Bretton Woods agreement, the United States committed itself, along with its fellow signatories, to a system of fixed exchange rates from which departure could be made only in exceptional circumstances of persistent fundamental disequilibrium. Only in such exceptional circumstances was a nation permitted to devalue or appreciate its currency, and then only under a system of rather strict procedural controls. In addition, the Bretton Woods agreement provided for the so-called special position of the U.S. dollar. First, it was established that a dollar was to consist of an ounce of gold of one thirty-fifth fineness, and also that any foreign central bank in the system had the right to convert dollars coming into its possession into gold at this fixed parity rate. In consequence, the American dollar was made ''as good as gold'' and thereby became a part of the official basic reserves of each of the foreign central banks. Thus, if a given central bank acquired additional dollars, it had the means to enlarge the stock of its own internal currency, using these reserves as a base. In the late 1960s, the system was modified further to provide for special drawing rights, based in part on currencies of the participating nations—the so-called paper gold.

Beginning in 1950, the United States started its twenty-year string of payments deficits; these deficits fed great quantities of dollars into the world, many of them ending up as central bank reserves in the countries holding them. The deficits were the source of Euro-dollars as well as of the central bank reserves of the countries participating in the system. As these foreign central banks undertook excessively expansionary monetary policies on the basis of their swollen and swelling official reserves, inflation spread all over the world. As the years went on, this system of fixed parities of exchange rates came under intolerable strains as inflation developed in country after country. By 1971, collapse of the system was at hand, when the United States slammed shut its "gold window" and refused to continue official conversion of dollars by foreign central banks. By early 1973, even the temporary structure of revised fixed parities proved unworkable, and the Western world found itself compelled to shift to floating rates.

Another part of the story starts in 1965 when the United States began raising its expenditures heavily for the war in Vietnam at the same time that it was substantially increasing outlays on the various Great Society programs. One consequence was accelerating inflation at home, which finally took double-digit form by 1973. Another was a veritable flood of dollars ending up in the inhospitable coffers of the central banks abroad. It should also be borne in mind that deficit financing of the federal budget, taking on formidable proportions, aggregated over $100 billion between fiscal 1965 and fiscal 1974. This was the domestic counterpart of the U.S. international payments deficit, in that it became the source for our ever-enlarging monetary base and the accelerating inflation that the base made possible.

To put the matter very briefly, the money supply in the hands of the American people grew at a rate of about 7½ percent a year over the past decade. Serious and very competent students of money, now called "monetarists," point out that if currency plus demand deposits expand at a rate of 7½ percent in a country where real gross output can have a trend rate of increase of only about 4 to 4¼ percent, serious and accelerating inflation will be the inevitable result.

The overall outcome has been a progressive overvaluation of the U.S. dollar during 1950–71. One result has been an upward surge in imports during this same period. Equally important, American exports were proving harder and harder to sell, reflecting as they did rising prices together with the continuing parity rate for the dollar relative to all the other nations in the Bretton Woods system. Increases in exports therefore developed a systematic and persisting sluggishness.

Impact of inflation on multinationals and home employment

Now, at last, we can look at the impact of this inflation on direct foreign investment by our multinationals and link it to home employment. Overvaluation of the dollar gradually became a powerful additional factor for attracting capital abroad, where production costs would be lower and the difficulties of exporting directly from the United States could be overcome. In addition, many multinationals were attracted to foreign production of things that could be returned to the United States as imports, again as an alternative to making the same goods here at home. In both respects, the potential consequence is reduced employment opportunities, and indeed in some cases, absolute reductions in employment itself. More than this, the fixed parity of the dollar relative to foreign currencies made it attractive for a multinational corporation to take overvalued dollars and to convert them into undervalued marks, for example, thus making a profit by converting capital to foreign form. The absence of a free market in foreign exchange, caused by maintaining unrealistic rates of conversion against the dollar, constituted a direct invitation to invest capital abroad.

Another element in this situation worthy of emphasis is that the fixed parity rates made it possible to manipulate trade to the disadvantage of the United States. Through an intricate system of direct restrictions on imports into Japan, the Japanese were able to build up a very substantial trade surplus with the United States, ultimately reaching over $6 billion a year. In a free market, this huge surplus would have depressed the dollar relative to the yen and would have made U.S. imports from Japan much more expensive, therefore less attractive, at the same time that U.S. exports to Japan would have been made much cheaper, therefore much more attractive to Japanese buyers. But the Bank of Japan, notwithstanding this great trade imbalance, protected the fixed rate of conversion between the yen and the dollar by the simple device of buying surplus dollars on the exchange market from Japanese exporters to the United States and stuffing the proceeds into the vaults of the central bank. Advantageously, this kept the yen cheap and the dollar dear. There are other instances of this same type of currency manipulation against the dollar. Together they help to explain the surge of imports and the flagging growth of our exports during the later 60s. In turn, these phenomena influenced the slowing growth of jobs and, in some particular industries, even the absolute decline in jobs. Faced with these trade disadvantages, multinationals in the United States found themselves compelled to look for ways to survive in various industries. The obvious solution was to set up branch fabricating and assembly plants somewhere in the Southeast Asian group of industrial countries, which was done.

One of the consequences is that beginning in 1965 the American labor movement adopted an increasingly protectionist stance. This took extreme form in labor's support for the Burke-Hartke bill then pending in Congress, which proposed, in effect, to eliminate the freedom of domestic multinational companies to export capital for direct investment abroad, and to eliminate their freedom to license the export of their technologies as well. More than this, the measure would have set up a system of import quotas to restrict the inflow of competing foreign goods. Thus one can fairly say that the outcome of this malign combination of a system of fixed parities of exchange and of domestic inflation in the United States was introduction of the most protectionist piece of legislation proposed since mercantilist times.

The Problem of Job Loss

But how big is the problem of actual job loss? To get at an answer, it is necessary to break down the problem into its parts. Each import of anything can be abstractly considered as a replacement for alternative production at home and, in this sense, as a cause of reduction in potential jobs. If there is full employment, of course, such an import causes no real loss of jobs unless the purpose is to make the product here even if it requires diverting labor from making something else—a factor usually overlooked in the argument against imports. If one pursues this policy of eliminating dependence on all imports, he ends up making things he ought to buy from his foreign partners and making less of the things he can easily sell to them or that he can make more cheaply for himself. This is a crude way of talking about the principle of "comparative advantage." If every nation followed this principle literally, of course, there would be no international trade, and all of the countries involved would have less real income for their people.

In looking at the job-loss problem, we start with the list of imports as such and use an input-output grid to separate the list into three parts: those items we cannot replace by home production—for example, chrome; those items that could be made at home but only at a cost so high it would be absurd to do so as long as they can be bought much more cheaply abroad; and a large and diverse group of imports that feasibly could be made at home at reasonable cost. These last products diverge among themselves as to the labor coefficients required to make them. Next, proceeding item by item, we look at this list of imports to see which increased and which decreased, and compare the respective amounts of labor involved to net out the number of potential jobs which provisionally may have been gained or lost by the changes in the volume of imports from year to year. We do the same thing in reverse for exports, looking at the components of exports to determine their labor coefficients, and then to estimate the number of jobs involved when exports increase or decrease. The third step is to look at jobs involved in supporting the export industries—for example, transportation, insurance, and banking services. Then the job changes associated with import changes in the net can be compared with the job changes associated with export changes in the net, so that comparisons can be made to find out whether these trade changes have made a difference in actual employment.

Lawrence Krause of the Brookings Institution made such an inquiry recently and found that for the 1970–71 recession there was a loss of only 17,000 jobs from trade change of these types. By contrast, total unemployment increased by more than 1.5 million in the same period, not because of changes in imports and exports, but through a total decline of effective demand. Thus the trade factor turned out to be trivial. And there is good reason to believe that it usually is trivial, that the control of unemployment can be accomplished neither efficiently nor adequately by attempts to interfere with the course of foreign trade.

Putting the same matter a little differently, the problem of unemployment in the United States is not a problem of foreign imports, nor is it a problem of losing exports. The real problem is inflation. Inflation fosters imports and at the same time cripples exports. Since early 1973 we alleviated the adverse impact of inflation by introducing the system of floating exchange rates in place of the old fixed parity arrangements. This denies our trading partners the opportunity to manipulate foreign trade to our disadvantage by operations in the foreign exchange market that would preserve the fixed parity of the dollar to their home currencies. (To be sure, there is a tactic known as the "dirty float" that still allows this game to be played up to a point, but not to the extent that prevailed before floating rates were introduced.)

The connection between higher unemployment and inflation is intricate. Although we do not have time to explore the subject at length here, what can be said is that inflation is always caused by excessive creation of money. In this way money incomes are increased all around, demands for goods then rise, inventories are drawn down, prices begin rising, and businessmen increase their demands, first for loan credit and later for long-term investment credits as well. The rising demand for credit increases interest rates, which in turn threatens to abort the boom. If the central bank then pumps in more reserves to permit the credit banks to extend more credits and supposedly in this manner to reduce interest rates, the inflation accelerates and interest rates rise in response. The ultimate crash has been put off, but only for a time.

If, instead, the central bank decides to break the inflation now, it will refuse to expand bank reserves. Eventually the money supply and prices stop rising, both consumption and investment demands begin dropping in real terms. Production plans are then cut back all around, layoffs begin and hiring declines. A general rise of unemployment is the direct consequence. This is what has been happening since the middle of 1974.

There is no way to stop inflation that would permit us to avoid an increase in unemployment. Obviously it is desirable to hold that increase to the minimum. But in accepting this minimum increase in unemployment, we should not overlook the much more important fact that many classes of the population suffer even greater losses through sustained inflation—the 22 million people who are 65 years old or more and who can not increase their money incomes; the 15 million people on welfare payments, whose incomes invariably fall behind the rise in prices; and 75 million wage and salary workers who cannot hope to raise their incomes as rapidly as the price level has been rising in the past two years. Thus inflation is not a problem just for rich people—it hits everybody.

The other point that must be stressed is that the cure for both inflation and high unemployment is better management of money itself. Emphatically, no solution to these problems can be found in protectionist legislation such as the Burke-Hartke bill. It is wholly understandable why certain unions would like to see this bill passed. These are unions whose base is in the import-competing industries and, to a lesser extent, in certain export trades. They feel the direct impact of trade changes, and they do not associate these trade changes with inflation and overvaluation of the dollar. But, while we may sympathize with the problems they confront, we are not obligated to accept a solution that is neither efficient nor adequate.

To sum up, the multinational corporation has a large and constructive place in a world-wide system of private enterprise. These concerns have fostered trade and diffusion of technology and managerial know-how to the benefit of many different countries, especially of their consuming populations. Indeed, we could even contend that the multinationals have made an indispensable contribution to the industrialization of many areas of the world itself. To be sure there are certain problems of international policy and of national sovereignty that have come up in connection with the spread of the multinational concerns, but these problems are not enormous, nor are they insoluble. Above all, they should not be interpreted as supporting the claims of socialists, whose real target is not the multinational corporation as such, but private profit-seeking enterprise everywhere.

MULTINATIONAL CORPORATIONS AND UNDERDEVELOPED COUNTRIES

HARRY MAGDOFF

In dealing with the multinational corporation we should begin by clarifying what we mean by this term. What is a multinational corporation? What is especially unique about these firms? The best way to answer is to put the phenomenon in historical perspective, to trace its roots and discern what particular aspects of the economic and social environment favored its blossoming into a major institution of contemporary capitalist society.

But while we dwell on the distinctive elements of this development we must not ignore the fact that basic economic impulses are equally at work before and after it. In many respects, the onset of the age of the multinational is a case of *plus ça change, plus c'est la même chose*. Indeed, multinationals represent a new stage in the fulfillment of essential driving forces of capitalist enterprise.

Basic trends of capitalism

The growth imperative. The need to grow is built into the nature of capitalist undertakings. Apart from the psychological conditioning of entrepreneurs in a social environment which measures sucess by the amount of wealth accumulated, higher profits (via improved profit rates and larger sales) actually must be pursued unceasingly, if only as a safeguard against the risk and uncertainty of a market economy. This necessity produces its own inner momentum: a healthy growth pattern must be produced to attract additional capital investment for still further growth. An additional incentive to persistent growth comes from the competitive struggle. Either because of aggressive, innovative action by a rival firm, or in anticipation of intrusion on its preserve, each corporation must, for security's sake alone, search for new products, new markets, and more effective marketing techniques, thus stimulating a rising spiral of investment, sales, and profits.

Spread and influence of giant corporations. The central tendency of the competitive struggle, occurring as it does in the midst of wide, cyclical business swings, is towards an increasing concentration of economic power in the hands of a relatively small number of gigantic firms; the weaker competitors are either eliminated or absorbed in bigger and stronger units. This does not mean the end of competition, however. A dynamic capitalist society has considerable turnover as new firms enter (to take advantage of inventions, discoveries, changes in style, and opportunities afforded by wars and business-cycle upturns) while others die out, thus keeping a certain degree of competition alive, especially among smaller and medium-size firms and in industries that are geared to local markets or to frequent changes in fashion. Even with this flux the drift is towards further concentration. Yet in those industries dominated by giant firms, pure monopoly rarely emerges because none of these giants is big or daring enough to risk everything in an attempt to destroy other giants. Competition remains a way of life even for the huge business establishments, but it is conducted with game rules appropriate to the increasing concentration of power.

Expanding on a world scale. Capitalism is in effect a world economy. Historically it has spread insistently beyond national borders and increasingly integrated as much of the globe as possible into this world economy. In fact, capitalism was born in a commercial revolution during which a world market was created for the products of Western Europe, on the one hand, and, on the other, food and raw materials for the emerging industrial centers were obtained from all over the world. As the industrial revolution expanded and led to further rapid technological changes, capitalist enterprise began to rely increasingly on world markets to dispose of the new products and the flow of mass-produced goods for which domestic demand, albeit rising, was insufficient. Thus, uneven development of industrializing nations, colonialism, and various forms of informal empire from time to time injected new vitality in industrial metropolitan centers, stimulating another upsurge in enterprise, another advance in sales, and another boost to profits. In this long process of international integration there evolved economic and social structures that encompassed the world.

Historical Setting

In the final analysis, then, the key trends that coalesce and ripen in the multinational corporation are the need to expand, the increasing concentration of economic power, and the urge to operate on a world scale. But the multinational does not suddenly appear as a full-fledged entity on the scene. Certain preconditions are necessary to its development: administrators need time to learn how to operate a business in a foreign environment; the firms must be well organized, and large enough to operate efficiently in a truly international fashion; and foreign political and economic relations must be favorable. To advance this argument, we need to understand the differences between two major stages of capitalist development—competitive and monopoly capitalism—and the special conditions arising after the Second World War which provided a hothouse for the burgeoning of the multinational.

Competitive capitalism

The main feature of competitive capitalism is, of course, an abundance of firms in each industry. In this situation, each firm tries to eliminate rivals and take a larger share of the market by reducing costs and then lowering prices. During this stage historically the western capital's main interest in the rest of the world was the search for new markets. Capital markets were maturing and U.S. entrepreneurs had made foreign investment. Both these developments became increasingly important in England, where the British railroad industry was fostered by loans and direct investment it used to build railway systems around the world. In still earlier days, British, Dutch, and other nationals from Western Europe developed plantations for the production of sugar, spices, etc. The drive for exports and investment penetration during the long era of competitive capitalism shaped the resulting world division of labor, with a periphery of so-called backward countries, often under colonial rule, becoming the providers of food and raw materials, and with a core of metropolitan centers, having superior military, financial, and industrial strength, supplying manufactured goods to the periphery. In balance, however, export of goods weighed much more heavily in determining this division of labor than did export of capital. External financing and foreign investment grew, but these instruments of capitalist expansion were merely in their infancy.

The monopoly stage and development of the multinational

Foreign investment came into its own during the monopoly stage of capitalism, which began in the last quarter of the nineteenth century. The awakening interest in capital exports was clearly associated with a qualitative leap forward in the concentration of economic power in the leading industrial nations. Although interrupted by two world wars and the Great Depression of the 1930s, foreign investment became increasingly important to the metropolitan centers. This overseas expansion of investment laid the foundations for the establishment of the multination-als after World War II. We can only highlight here some of the main rea-sons for this new departure in international economic relations.

First, at the heart of the new monopoly stage was the onset of a host of new industries based on major technological breakthroughs—for exam-ple: steel, electric power, oil refining, synthetic chemicals, aluminum, and the internal combustion engine industries which got a firm foothold in the latter decades of the nineteenth century. These new technologies necessitated giantism—large and complicated plants with industrial progress dependent on big investments in research and development. Hence they required mobilization of capital through financial markets and a consequent growth of powerful banks and other financial inter-mediaries.

Second, the growth of giant firms, due to the new technology or the elimination of competitors in the older industries, was accompanied by the emergence of new business strategy based on a striving for control. When you have three or four companies serving 60 to 80 percent of a market, control becomes both possible and necessary. Thus, control over raw material supplies provides a defensive as well as offensive weapon against competitors. Under these circumstances the nature of competition changes from one of outbidding rivals through price cuts to one of dominating market shares. Advertising, various forms of sales promotion, product differentiation, exclusive technology, and influence over distribution outlets provide the armament for securing market shares. And it is this thirst for, as well as the financial ability to, control which induces the new importance of foreign investment—investment which facilitates control over foreign sources of raw materials and over foreign markets.

Third, a corollary to this striving for control has been the increasing role of the state. Alongside the growth of the large corporation comes a spurt of militarism and colonial wars. Under the incentive of construct-ing navies and arming infantry, a number of governments provide needed financial support for the new giants, especially those in the more modern technological sector. In addition, the exercise of military power, or the threat of its use, creates new avenues for investment and trade, including enhanced opportunities for higher profits through operating plants in countries with exceptionally low wages.

Fourth, an outstanding feature of the monopoly stage is its challenge to Britain's formerly leading and dominant position in industrial, finan-cial, and military power. England's advantage of being the leader in the first industrial revolution of the eighteenth century became a relative disadvantage in the second industrial revolution at the end of the nineteenth century. France, Germany, the United States, and, some-what later, Japan were able to benefit from the new technology of industry and warfare without the drawbacks of an accumulation of obsolescent equipment. The ensuing rivalry of the advanced nations served to spur foreign investment. Competition among giant firms was no longer confined to a nation's own boundaries; it extended to large corporate enterprises of several countries. Penetration of international markets via exports became increasingly difficult as a wave of protective tariffs—tariffs not so much to protect infant industries as to safeguard the more advanced export-oriented industries—spread throughout the more advanced industrial nations. Thus, foreign investment in each other's preserves became a useful way to avoid tariff barriers as well as a device for better control over a share of the local market.

Here, in sum, we have the background for the new stage of foreign economic relations of the monopoly period: exports are still important, but foreign investment becomes increasingly significant, beginning to overreach exports as the main method of operating in the world economy. Prior to the First World War the main actors on this stage were England, France, and Germany. England's primacy in overseas economic activity during the era of competitive capitalism is reflected in the fact that until the First World War it accounted for 50 percent of all the foreign investment made by the leading industrial nations. France and Germany contributed another 40 percent. In this period the role of the United States, at that time still a debtor nation, was small potatoes. Nevertheless, some foreign investment did take place. A number of manufacturing firms with a decided technical advantage, as for example Singer Sewing and McCormick, moved out of their domestic limits to produce in other countries. In total, the foreign investment of the United States before World War I accounted for some six percent of the world's foreign investment.

Primacy of the United States

The changing fortunes resulting from the war turned these roles around substantially. The foreign investments of France and Germany became relatively unimportant in this sphere. Among other events, Germany's assets abroad were taken over by the victors, and France, as well as Germany and other investing nations, lost its holdings in Russia as a result of the Bolshevik Revolution. England, too, lost out, having to sell off foreign assets in order to finance the purchase of armaments. What we see then is a decline in the share of total foreign investment held by France and Germany from a combined percentage of 40 before the war to only 11 in the period between the First and Second World Wars. The growing challenge by the United States for leadership of the capitalist world is reflected in the changing position of the United States in this area. By the beginning of World War II, the U.S. share of foreign investment reached a healthy 35 percent.

While I cannot take the time on this occasion to expand on the causal interrelations of economic, political, and military power, it is worth mentioning in passing that we see here correlations which merit further investigation. The changing structure of the world economy after the Second World War further illustrates this correlation, for in recent decades the U.S. role in foreign investment as in international political and military affairs, has become paramount. By the early 1970s the United States accounted for 60 percent of all foreign investment in the capitalist world. The United Kingdom and France also participated in the increase in overseas investment, controlling about 20 percent between them. At the end of the Second World War the competitive positions of Germany and Japan were obviously devastated—Germany having lost its challenge for control of Europe and Japan's investments in China, Formosa, and Korea having evaporated. But while still relatively small contenders compared to the United States and England, the former losers, now full-fledged allies of the United States, are making a rapid comeback; between 1966 and 1971 Germany increased its foreign investments by over 170 percent, Japan by 270 percent.

The very rapid growth of U.S. foreign investment, and its foremost position in this area, laid the groundwork for the age of the multinationals. But first let me explain what I think were the chief reasons for the post–World War II explosion of U.S. foreign investment:

1. The United States became the center of the international money market and the primary international banker for the rest of the capitalist world. This development was facilitated by the Bretton Woods agreements, under which the U.S. dollar was accepted by other countries as if it were as good as gold. Thus, the United States was able to operate for at least two decades with a deficit in its balance of payments—a deficit which in effect financed the growth in foreign investment as well as global military operations and foreign military and economic aid.

2. The Marshall Plan, designed to reconstruct the Western European allies of the United States, directly and indirectly invigorated foreign investment. U.S. firms were involved directly in reconstruction efforts and opportunities which were thereby provided for establishing branches in the Marshall Plan countries. Paradoxically, this same economic aid also helped bring back giant competitors in European countries, thus indirectly spurring U.S. firms to establish themselves in Marshall Plan countries in pursuit of market control.

3. Extensive foreign aid programs in addition to the Marshall Plan provided the wherewithal for the purchase of U.S. goods, with the consequent penetration of many markets where consumers became

interested in U.S. products and the level of consumption rose. This development provided a sound base for starting foreign branches. In addition, in the administration of foreign aid American businessmen accumulated a great deal of practical experience and knowledge of inestimable value in running foreign business ventures—knowledge of languages, laws, customs, and contacts with the right people.

4. The Second World War galvanized major technological innovations which, together with government financing of defense production, helped create out of former giants supergiants, organizations that were more able to operate on a truly international scale than any others had been at any time in the past. Furthermore, government financing of research and development helped create advances in areas such as communication, computers, and aviation—the technological nucleus of multinational operation.

5. Events associated with the Second World War and its aftermath resulted in the elimination of some former restraints to the growth of foreign investment. Thus a number of former international cartels were dissolved. These cartels had established exclusive preserves and hence acted as a damper on foreign investment; the end of them opened up new territories for expansion. The barriers to entry in colonies disappeared with the decline of colonialism. Decolonization opened doors for U.S. foreign investment which formerly had been kept shut by the colonizing nations.

6. Preeminent among all the above, however, was the sense of security supplied to foreign as well as U.S. corporations created by the Pax Americana—a world capitalist order backed by the U.S. Air Force strategically positioned in bases around the globe, by other armed forces stationed in numerous countries, by military aid to support governments committed to the support of "free enterprise," by an active policy to suppress revolutionary and national liberation movements, and finally, by a stockpile of atomic bombs. From this contribution to law and order sprang confidence in a cooperative environment for the spread, by compulsion, of the multinationals.

The United States was clearly the foremost leader in both the rapid postwar expansion of foreign investment and the new multinational form of international operation. But as the other industrialized nations recovered from the ruins of war, they too began to participate actively, for, apart from their own inner needs to grow and to capture foreign markets, they had to meet the competitive threat from U.S. firms. Some notion of the magnitude and impact of the multinationals can be grasped from key data for 1971 given in a recent report of a United Nations special committee. According to its study, the top ten multinational corporations each produced a value added of over $3 billion dollars—that is larger than the gross national product of 80 different countries. All the multinational corporations together produced goods worth $500 billion in 1971, which represents one-fifth the total manufacturing production in all the capitalist countries. Finally, the total output of the subsidiaries of multinational corporations—in other words, what they produce away from home—is now greater than the export trade of the capitalist nations.

Multinationals' Effect on the Third World

Characteristics of the multinational

Intertwined with the impressive growth and economic impact of the multinationals are two fairly new features which distinguish them from former types of international investment. First is the number of countries in which these firms have sunk their roots. In the earlier days of international investment, even during the decades of expansion from the end of the nineteenth century to the Second World War, the typical international corporation ran one, two, or three overseas subsidiaries. Characteristic of the multinational now, however, is to own branches in at least six countries and often in more than a dozen widespread locations. Thus today there are 200 corporations, among the largest in the world, having branches in twenty or more countries.

The second important difference is the new financial strategy of maximizing profits globally. Before the multinational type of operation evolved, each foreign subsidiary was more or less on its own. If the branch plant couldn't make a go of it in the host country, it was closed. This has changed. The modern approach is to treat the world-wide operations as part of a unified economic and financial organism. The usefulness of a particular branch is now measured not merely in terms of the direct profits arising from its own operations but by its contribution to the combined profits of the multinational. The activities of the various subsidiaries become integrated into a global strategy, supported by the advance in air transport, communications, and computer technology. With increased speed in travel available to executives, instantaneous and relatively inexpensive communication possible between branches, and the ability to amass and analyze a tremendous amount of data at its command, the financial center in the national headquarters of the multinational corporation can control the destinies of the far-flung enterprises in its pursuit of global profit maximization. This new level of integrated operations is graphically summarized by a former chairman of General Motors Corporation:

> If the South African assembly operation of General Motors, and its recently added manufacturing facilities, are to function smoothly and efficiently, they must today receive a carefully controlled and coordinated flow of vehicle parts and components from West Germany, England, Canada, the

> United States, and even Australia. These must reach General Motors South Africa in the right volume and at the right time to allow an orderly scheduling of assembly without excessive accumulation of inventories. This is a challenging assignment which must be made to work if the investment is to be a profitable one.

Thus, the success of the South African branch depends not merely on the local operations but on coordination of activities around the globe. And, while General Motors and all other multinationals will seek to make each subsidiary as profitable as possible, the measure of their success can be considerably moderated by the mutual support required from the different segments.

Strategies of multinationals in third world countries

These new and distinguishing features of the multinationals—global extension and global profit maximization—have also been reflected in changing strategies in the third world. Before the onset of the multinationals the central interest of foreign investment in the underdeveloped countries was in extractive industries, notably for control over the supply of raw materials. Investment in other industries, such as manufacturing and public utilities, was relatively limited and usually confined to a country's colonial empire (e.g., the British in India) or sphere of special influence (e.g., the United States in Latin America). The interest in extractive industries of course remains, although tempered by growing nationalism in the third world. But added to it is a reawakened interest in establishing manufacturing subsidiaries in these countries. Behind this new departure is the Pax Americana, noted previously, and the contributions to infrastructure (roads, harbors, electric power, etc.) made by World Bank financing and by aid from the United States and other investing countries. Also important are the so-called rising expectations held by formerly colonial and semi-colonial areas. The desire to industrialize opened new opportunities for foreign investors, which were often encouraged by cooperative gestures of host countries in the form of tax and other incentives.

The novel character of the multinationals also helped. These supergiants' ability to function successfully over great distances and in strange environments stimulated greater responsiveness to the profit-making potentials in the third world than in the past. Furthermore, the changed financial strategy widened the options for desirable new locations. Once the test for success shifted from the performance of each separate part to the contribution that each part makes to a global system of production and distribution, many third world locations which had formerly been deemed undesirable suddenly became especially attractive, not the least of their attractions being their lower living standards and, hence, the incredibly low wages that their factory operatives could be paid.

We can note two phases of this increasing attention to manufacturing in the underdeveloped nations. At first, the main emphasis was on manufactured goods which previously had been imported. This import substitution approach worked up to certain inhibiting limits because of the relatively small multiplier effect of these investments and because of restricted domestic markets. As the third world countries began to recognize the limited aspects of import-substitution as the key to development, and as they became more conscious of the constraints imposed by their reliance on exporting a few extractive-industry products, they began to realize that more successful growth must be encouraged by exporting manufactured goods. During the first phase the more aggressive underdeveloped countries encouraged investments in the manufacture of parts and components for existing assembly (or packaging) plants as well as production of finished consumer goods which traditionally had been imported. In the second phase, developing nations put greater emphasis on attracting foreign investment in manufacturing products that would enter world trade channels. Each of these strategies met favor in the central offices of the multinationals. But the multinationals have handled export-oriented investments by creating export platforms in selected countries where cheap labor and export facilities were unusually attractive—South Korea, Formosa, Hong Kong, and Singapore.

Benefits and shortcomings: three views

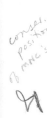

With the spread of multinationals and their broadening spheres of activity in the third world we have been witnessing intensified controversy over the nature and significance of their operations. The conservative view in this controversy, and probably the main stream of orthodox thinking, is that the multinational impact on the underdeveloped economies is positive, probably even essential for their successful economic development. The size and integrated global patterns of multinational firms contain much of benefit: the ability to tap financial, physical, and human resources from major parts of the world; competence to combine these resources in economically feasible and profitable undertakings; production and managerial ability to translate resources into specific outputs; and the capacity to transfer the most advanced technology and most competent skills. Conservatives recognize that such capacities can also have negative effects, indicated by the underhanded dealings of IT&T in Chile, for example. But the very giantism of the multinationals, their access to science and research, and their flexibility in moving people and capital from one area to another all add up to an invaluable tool for social progress, one that, in the conservative view, far outweighs noticeable shortcomings.

Liberals grant the essential validity of the conservative argument, but feel that it justifies the negative effects too easily. The control exercised by the multinationals in weak, backward nations should not be glossed over, they argue. Even when these international establishments operate fairly, their sheer power is bound to overwhelm most underdeveloped countries. Consider the comparative bargaining strength of a typical multinational and a country whose economic resources are smaller than those of the company itself. The liberals also claim that while the multi-nationals at first make significant contributions to third world countries, after a certain point is reached they begin to have negative effects. In time the foreign firm takes out more (in the form of profits, royalties, and managerial fees) than it has brought in. On the basis of this evaluation, liberals believe the good aspects of the multinationals should be encour-aged and the bad should be suppressed. The excesses can be curbed by international supervision, improved antitrust laws, more informed bar-gaining by host countries, and nationalization (with adequate compensa-tion) of those firms which have passed from promoting progress to hold-ing it back.

The dominant radical position in the multinational controversy does not deny the technical competence of the multinational firms nor their capability in transferring useful technology. However, these critics take the shortcomings of foreign investment much more seriously than do the liberals, and hence conclude that underdeveloped countries would be better off without such investment. A great deal of attention is paid in their bill of particulars to the power multinationals exercise to support reactionary and oppressive regimes. Radicals also argue that because of the necessary concentration on profitability, the multinationals invest in areas which are not necessarily advantageous to the welfare of the host country, ignoring key needs of development. Further, because of their economic power, the foreign firms have first call on the financial re-sources of the host countries, thus restricting opportunities for domestic capitalists. The advanced technology brought in from abroad is highly mechanized, and therefore does not contribute to solving the severe un-employment problem common to the third world. In the search for ever greater profits these firms are bound to manipulate transfer prices and indirect forms of return on capital as well as direct repatriation of profits so as to create constraints on the domestic economic surplus that might otherwise be devoted to essential development needs. Finally, develop-ing nations' very dependence on foreign technology reflects a slew of re-lations which create a continuous burden of debt, hence political obliga-tion, to the metropolitan center—all of which deter independent and rapid growth.

Flowing from this radical analysis is the recommendation that the third world countries would best serve their own interests by getting rid of the multinationals: nationalize and, if feasible, confiscate the existing foreign investments and prohibit new investments from foreign countries. Japan is often cited as a prime example of a country that succeeded in industrializing largely because foreign firms were excluded.

At this point I should explain that there are two variants to the radical position. Many radicals blame multinationals for the state of underdevelopment. They therefore conclude that exclusion of the multinationals will initiate a series of events favorable to successful growth patterns. The second variant of the radical critique, one with which I associate myself, is that eliminating the multinationals is a necessary but not a sufficient condition for escape from the trap of poverty. Class structure and its accompanying socioeconomic development stay the same if elimination of foreign capital is the only reform. The ties that bind the economy to the dominant metropolitan centers remain. And the social psychology of dependence and inferiority are not significantly altered as long as the old social structure and the traditional links to the trade and finance of imperialism remain. Hence, the problem, as this second radical view sees it, is to change the power relations in the society—a change that brings the former oppressed classes into power and with it a change in priorities aimed at meeting the basic needs of the impoverished and downtrodden.

The argument to counter this second position is that such a program will not succeed because what the underdeveloped countries need most is technology and capital. Bad as the multinationals may be, they at least bring in the foreign exchange, the technology, and the know-how which make it possible to get out of the cycle of impoverishment.

Analysis of the traditional view

Let us analyze this rebuttal. As to capital, I think it is about time we discard the myth that foreign investment brings capital to the third world. When a new investment is made by outsiders there is obviously an inflow of capital. The inflow is usually not as large as generally pictured, for the simple reason that foreign resources usually contribute only a minor share of the investment. In entirely new ventures, the outside investor contributes capital primarily for equity ownership. But a considerable amount of financing is done through debt capital, and more often than not this capital comes from the resources of the host country. In the case of expansions of existing ventures the capital contribution from abroad is even smaller. For here not only does the host country supply debt capital, but also funds generated by already existing investment (depreciation reserves and a portion of the profits) in the host country. In such instances the capital from abroad is as a rule only a minor portion of the investment.

The real story, however, is in the overall balance of the capital flow. While each new bundle of foreign investment injects some new capital, this investment represents a claim on the capital generated in the home country consisting of dividends returned to the center from which the investment originated plus a variety of other payments, such as royalties on patents and trademarks, management fees, license fees, overpayments on raw materials and components imported from the mother company, and the like. In strict balance-of-payments terms the repatriated funds are treated as income, not capital. This is tenable terminology from the view of the investing country, not from the standpoint of the host country. Aside from technology and know-how, the supposed benefit of foreign investment is the addition it makes to badly needed foreign exchange. But the underdeveloped nation also must have investment financing from internal savings (or surplus). From both the balance-of-payment and investment-of-savings approaches, the flow of returns on foreign invested capital to the multinational offsets the foreign capital entering the country and drains domestically produced savings. Thus, the claims of foreign investments are, in effect, a capital outflow.

As seen from this outlook, the net balance in the flow of capital to and from investing countries has been, and continues to be, in favor of the investing country, not of the host country. The data on this are very clear. The outflow from the underdeveloped countries in the form of dividends, interest on loans, management, and license and royalty fees has been considerably larger than the inflow of equity and loan capital. While one may argue that certain types of foreign investment bring other benefits, it should be clear that the burden on local savings which might otherwise go into domestic investment and on foreign exchange is far in excess of the capital contribution made by the inflow from abroad.

The second element of the counter argument, i.e., the question about technology, taken in its broadest sense, is quite another matter. Here we come up against a real issue that must be taken seriously, a fundamental about which conservatives, liberals, and radicals have similar opinions. All agree that the problem of underdevelopment is not solely one of great inequities in the distribution of the national product. What is most urgently needed is a great increase in total production. For this it is essential to put idle hands to work and to increase the amount of goods each worker turns out in a given period. On both scores, but especially in the matter of increasing productivity, better equipment and increased application of technical knowledge is needed. The dissenting viewpoints part company with the traditional approach over the two subsumptions of the reigning orthodoxy: (1) The science and technology needed in the underdeveloped world can *only* be transferred by foreign investors who have a profit incentive; and (2) in any event, the multinationals, despite their shortcomings, are the most efficient channel for bringing in this technology.

The first point, that foreign investment is the only source of modern technology, has been proved false by history. Japan, the Soviet Union, North Korea, and China have all demonstrated that an underdeveloped nation can speedily obtain, exploit, and adapt modern science and technology without major dependence on foreign investment. The technical assistance which these countries received from foreign capitalists came by way of contracts for specific projects initiated by the host country, which avoided the deleterious effects of such investments— perpetual ownership and profit-taking by the foreign entrepreneurs.

Underlying both of the above subsumptions is the fallacy of a crude technological determinism. One need not neglect the crucial role of technology to dispute an oversimplified technological determinism which assumes that a more modern and improved technology will inevitably, and almost automatically, produce conforming social changes. A domestic social agent is needed for social change; specifically, a social class that has a vital interest in pursuing and utilizing innovations, as well as the will and the power to implement this interest. In the absence of such an agent and the proper environment in which the agency can flex its muscles, the best of science and technology may lie fallow.

The thinking behind this technological determinism also ignores an important distinction between precapitalist technical developments and the fruits of capitalism. In general, the state of the technical arts in each stage of development determines both the potential opportunities for production and its limits. Looking broadly at the long stretch of history prior to capitalism we see that the limitations were more important than the potential. Through almost all of history, the standard of living of the majority of the world's population was severely restricted despite the many revolutionary advances in methods of production and transportation. However, although one can speculate on how much better past societies might have been with better organization of economic activity or with a more equitable distribution of output, the basic reality remains that even with the best will and the most altruistic of rulers, the people's living conditions would not have been significantly improved. The constraints on the production potential imposed by available knowledge and tools were too rigid.

With the industrial revolution, however, the possibilities changed dramatically. A body of scientific knowledge, not to mention a stockpile of tools and the ability to reproduce tools on an expanding scale, has been generated which opens up entirely new horizons for the living standards of the people of the world. Limits are clearly and most decidedly present, as no doubt they will always be. The difference today is that the potential carries more weight than the limits. The room for choice has been vastly enlarged. In contrast with the past, when certain types of social development were circumscribed by barriers of knowledge, the limits imposed by the prevailing arts are less important. Society can, if it wishes, select from a wide variety of technologies and with many more degrees of freedom in its choice of priorities. Thus, even though technology still imposes certain limits and restricts the range of choice, what is most important today, in fact decisive, is the agent of change: Who is in charge and for what purpose?

This brings us to the second of the traditionalists' subsumptions about technology mentioned above—the multinationals are the most efficient and reliable transferers of technology. If the existing class structures in the third world are to be more or less maintained, if production is to be geared to meeting the effective demand of the top income groups, and if improvement in the living conditions of the unemployed and the miserable peasant masses are to rely on the eventual trickling-down of some of the income from the top—then by all means the job can best be done by the multinationals. Although one might insist, as many liberals do, that the claws of the multinationals be trimmed and their greed be curbed somewhat, nevertheless, if what is called for is industry to supply the needs and desires of the upper strata, it is reasonable to expect that the multinationals will select the most suitable way of producing the required goods at the lowest cost. Moreover, this transfer of technology will most likely multiply opportunities for local elites to further enrich themselves. If these benefits are insufficient for the native upper classes—if they are seeking new sources of profit from, say, exports— then the multinationals will benefit them still further. After all, the multinationals know what will prosper in world trade and how to develop entry into new markets.

Let us suppose, on the other hand, that there is a reversal of class power in the third world—one which results in control by a ruling class, or alliance of classes, that insists on a totally different set of priorities. For example, giving first and absolute priority to improving the lot of the impoverished majority of the population by eliminating hunger and epidemic diseases, raising housing and clothing standards, bringing medical services to the poor and dispersed, and, introducing education and cultural opportunities for all the people, not just the privileged. The science and technology to achieve these goals exists, but it is not the technology that the multinationals offer. Nor are these firms suited to select the most appropriate technology to meet the above-listed needs, competent as they are to meet the demand patterns in a capitalist society.

us more in agriculture where most needed.

Technology and the needs of third-world societies

Before considering the sort of industrial arts needed with these alternate objectives we should recall that there are two means of increasing national output: 1) full and nonwasteful use of the labor supply, and 2) a growth in labor productivity. The multinationals have little to offer with respect to the first requirement. Their technology is capital intensive; the resulting absorption of the unemployed is therefore minor. Their competent engineers and production managers would be at a loss in designing and directing programs for rapid absorption of the unemployed and underemployed in the most essential projects, because what is needed is a social and political mobilization of the people putting them to work on groundwork essential to advance agriculture and improved health; i.e., water conservancy projects, irrigation networks, latrines, sewers, roads, canals, inoculation against epidemic diseases, and similar endeavors. This involves a redirection of domestic physical resources and a mobilization of the domestic population, neither of which is in the domain or competence of a profit-seeking corporation. It is true, of course, that these firms can offer very helpful equipment and machinery to accomplish the urgent tasks more quickly. But most of the required jobs will not be started, because poor countries haven't the means to pay for the importation or domestic manufacture of sufficient technical aids to wipe out hunger and epidemic disease quickly. Relying on such machinery and waiting until all that is needed is available will divert resources from the main tasks, with the likelihood that poverty will increase still further during the wait.

The multinationals do not have much to offer in the technical arts and means for raising labor productivity and increasing agricultural yields, either. What is most urgently called for—remembering the context of the new priorities—are such implements as vast quantities of wooden and metal carts, wheelbarrows, and bicycles to replace the movement of goods on head or shoulder; cement to waterproof linings of irrigation systems and drains; pumps, pipes, and sprinkling apparatus for irrigation; silos; and simple hand and mechanical devices for plowing, weeding, and threshing. In this kind of production, the standards of industrial organization and efficiency would differ radically from those of the multinationals. Thus the remedy for unemployment in rural areas, as well as the need to overcome inadequate transportation facilities, is to be found in widely dispersed, small and medium-sized plants. This sort of technology and plant organization is directly opposite to what would be designed according to the cost and profit calculations of big business.

At the heart of the dispute between those who place their confidence in the transfer of technology and those who stress self-reliance is the issue of technology versus people. The former believe that technology is the more important ingredient, and that the fastest way of achieving higher levels of technology is with the entry and expansion of the multinational firm. The latter claim that people are more important than imported technology. Where there are large numbers of underutilized or unemployed workers along with inadequate capital, the major task becomes one of substituting labor for capital. In the abstract it may seem that there is no contradiction in doing both: importing capital and mobilizing domestic labor supply for the most urgent needs. In reality, though, the contradiction exists, since the job of mobilizing labor requires a political decision and highly centralized planning—both of which conflict sharply with the profit motive of private enterprise.

The issue of technology versus people goes even deeper. The people of the former colonial and semi-colonial nations suffer not only from poverty but from various forms of psychological enslavement: the sense of inferiority to the "masters" of the technologically advanced centers, plus all the marks of oppression by native ruling classes, including reliance on superstition instead of science, lack of confidence in self-development, and subservience to those in power. As long as these psychological burdens remain, the best technology will have limited effect on the well-being of the people. Thus, it is not tractors, reapers, and threshers that are of the first order of importance in coping with the food shortages in these countries. On the contrary, improvement in agricultural yields depends on (a) removing the yoke of the landlord and local money lender, and (b) a revolutionary change in the peasants' thinking. Education, dissemination of technical information, ability of farmers to read and to calculate—this is the primary "technology" needed. We are talking about a social revolutionary change where agricultural science is not the exclusive property of technicians and agribusiness but instead moves into the domain of the everyday farmer.

Similar considerations apply to manufacturing. More important than the transfer of technology by outsiders is the achievement of native mastery over design and research. Mass education of mechanics, covering not only school education on technical matters but extensive practice as well, has to come first if a country is ever to rid itself of the yoke of dependency on foreign technology. This may take a long time, and undoubtedly will entail the delays common to the trial-and-error approach, but the alternative is a much longer period of reliance on foreign technicians. Once a country develops an indigenous ability to design and develop machines, then it is in a position to borrow and adapt what is required by its own circumstances and its own social policy objectives.

The course of self-reliance does not mean autarky. We are not talking about elimination of foreign trade or absolute isolation from the multinationals. At issue here is one of mastery. The traditional rules of the game—the existing price/wage relations, the established composition of foreign trade, the transfer of technology via foreign investment—serve to reproduce the basic patterns of poverty and ultimate subservience to the needs and profit drives of the more advanced nations. The road to independence and solution of the most crucial human problems can only be paved by radical changes in these game rules. If the objective is to give first priority to overcoming hunger and disease, then the people must become the masters of their destiny. Towards such a goal, a social revolution must precede the technological revolution.

TAXATION AND PROTECTION OF MULTINATIONAL CORPORATIONS: AMERICAN POLICY TODAY AND TOMORROW

G. C. HUFBAUER

Taxation

The U.S. Treasury extends its reach further than the finance ministries of most industrial countries. Ever since the Income Tax Act of 1913, the United States has claimed the right to tax the world-wide income of its citizens and corporations. What considerations have guided Congress in using this world-wide taxing power?

Cardinal Richelieu once remarked that the art of taxation is the art of plucking the goose with the least possible squawk. People in high places still pay heed to the Cardinal's advice. But in recent years fiscal experts have increasingly taken public compliance and revenue collections for granted. The major policy debate has been waged between advocates of neutral and equitable taxation on the one hand and proponents of functional taxation on the other. This debate has touched every branch of the tax law. Just as architects differentiate aesthetics and function, so do fiscal experts argue between abstract principles and functional goals. Let me illustrate this debate as it applies in the field of international taxation.

Neutral and equitable taxation

Neutral taxation is that mode of taxation which exerts the least possible impact on the private decisions of what goods to produce, how to produce them, where to locate production, and who shall be producers. To some extent, all taxation distorts the market place. In particular, the corporate income tax discriminates against capital-intensive goods and techniques. What role, then, can the concept of neutrality play in the in-

49

ternational taxation of corporate income?

While corporate income taxation necessarily affects the type of goods made and the technique of production, it can be designed to leave unchanged the location of production and the identity of producers. If a firm pays a corporate tax of 48 percent in the United States but only 42 percent in Belgium, it may shift manufacturing facilities from the United States to Belgium. The locational nonneutrality of the tax system could be averted if both nations imposed the same corporate tax rate.

The United States cannot unilaterally achieve tax harmonization. If the United States and Belgium agreed on a 45 percent corporate rate, that compromise would accentuate the disparity between the United States tax rate and the United Kingdom's 50 percent tax rate. The most the United States can unilaterally accomplish is to tax all U.S. corporations at the same rate, so that their locational decisions as between the United States and foreign nations are not biased by taxation. However, if the United States taxes its corporations operating in Belgium at 48 percent, then American firms will be disadvantaged by comparison with Belgian firms. The result will be nonneutrality as to the identity of producers. The United States cannot simultaneously achieve neutrality in both the location and identity of producers. Quite often, as in this example, one kind of neutrality can be reached only at the expense of another kind of neutrality.

Tax equity requires that taxpayers in like circumstances pay taxes on an equal footing.[1] The definition of like circumstances is elusive. Each taxpayer can plausibly be compared with many other taxpayers. The U.S. corporate subsidiary operating in Switzerland will naturally compare its tax burden with the tax burden of a Swiss competitor. But a U.S. senator might compare the tax burden of the Swiss subsidiary with the tax burden of the New Jersey subsidiary. The concept of equity covers much the same ground as, and raises many of the same conundrums as, the concept of neutrality. Equitable taxation for one bilateral relationship will often imply inequitable taxation for another bilateral relationship.

Nonetheless, the concepts of neutrality and equity have played an important role in shaping the tax code. Present United States taxation of American enterprise abroad embodies a mixture of capital-import neutrality, capital-export neutrality, and revenue protection clauses. The principles of national neutrality have so far exerted little effect on U.S. tax practice.[2]

Capital-import neutrality is achieved when firms of all nationalities operating in, for example, the Italian office equipment industry pay the same ultimate tax rate on their Italian profits. Pure capital-import neutrality would emerge if Italian tax and subsidy law made no distinction between enterprises of diverse national origin, and if foreign nations made no attempt to tax earnings arising in Italy. Firms of diverse national origin could then compete on an equal tax basis, thereby promoting the most efficient use of host country resources.

Capital-export neutrality is achieved when the enterprise pays the same total rate of tax on either foreign or domestic profits. For example, if the French susidiary of a U.S. firm pays 40 percent of its profits in tax to France, and if the U.S. corporate tax rate is 48 percent, capital-export neutrality would be served by a current U.S. tax of 8 percent of the French profits. A regime of pure capital-export neutrality would encourage U.S. firms to locate their productive facilities wherever pre-tax returns promised to be greatest. Thus, the U.S. capital stock would be allocated in a manner designed to optimize *world* production.

National neutrality is designed to ensure that the total U.S. returns to capital, which are shared between the U.S. government (in the form of taxes) and U.S. citizens, remain the same whether the capital is located at home or abroad. The equality of total returns would be achieved if U.S. firms paid the same current rate of tax to the U.S. government regardless of where earnings arose. Foreign income taxes could be deducted from foreign earnings but not credited against U.S. tax. For example, if the firm earned $180 in Mexico and Mexican taxes were $80, it would pay a U.S. tax of $48 (48 percent of $100). Unless a given investment could earn greater post–foreign-tax returns abroad than pre-U.S. tax returns at home, the firm would have no incentive to go abroad. But national neutrality would enhance home country welfare by ensuring the same return to the American body politic whether its capital is placed in Indonesia or Indiana.[3]

Multinational firms not only shift capital from one part of the world to another, they are also, and perhaps more importantly, conduits for the transfer of technology. Yet the concepts of tax neutrality that I have been discussing were not designed with management fees and royalties in mind. The use of American technology does not deplete the stock of knowledge available for home application. It is still possible to speak of tax neutrality in terms of a division of taxing authority between sovereign nations, and a limit on overall taxation. But it is considerably more difficult to link a particular version of tax neutrality with a particular pattern of resource allocation and the consequent impact on national welfare.[4]

The keystone of U.S. taxation of American enterprise abroad is the foreign tax credit. Subject to limits, U.S. firms may take a credit against the tentative U.S. tax for the underlying foreign income tax levied either on the repatriated earnings of foreign corporate subsidiaries or on the total earnings of foreign branches of the U.S. corporation. Thus, if a U.S. firm repatriates dividends, interest, royalties, or management fees from its foreign corporate subsidiary or operates abroad in branch form, and if foreign tax rates are not too high, the foreign tax credit may come close to ensuring capital-export neutrality.[5]

When the earnings of a foreign corporate subsidiary are not remitted, U.S. tax practice comes close to achieving capital-import neutrality. No current U.S. tax is levied on those earnings.[6] Instead U.S. taxation is deferred until repatriation. Insofar as earnings are retained abroad, deferral places the American enterprise on much the same tax footing as its local competitor.

In essence, an American multinational enterprise can elect to have its foreign ventures taxed either under a modified form of capital-export neutrality or under a modified form of capital-import neutrality. In neither case are the rules pure, but by choosing between a foreign branch and a foreign corporate subsidiary form, and by altering its payout practices, the firm can significantly shift from one standard to another.

The 1972 revenue consequences of the tax code may be summarized briefly. Corporate pre-tax foreign earnings were about $23.7 billion; foreign taxes took about $12.0 billion (50.5 percent of pre-tax earnings), and the U.S. tax took about $1.2 billion (5.2 percent of pre-tax earnings). As these figures indicate, U.S. corporations pay substantial tax on their foreign income, but nearly all the revenue flows to foreign governments.

I have mentioned only some of the intricacies posed by neutrality and equity. Many congressmen grow impatient with these abstract fiscal principles. They are not so much concerned with the aesthetics of the tax system as with questions of resource allocation and income distribution.[7] Thus they turn to functional standards: taxation designed to achieve specific goals.

Functional taxation

In its crudest form, functional taxation means "tax your enemies and subsidize your friends." But functional taxation is usually dressed in more elegant rhetoric. In the 1950s and early 1960s, it was said that the tax laws ought to encourage foreign investment. Many hoped that private foreign investment could replace public foreign aid. Thus, the Treasury was urged to abandon all taxation of foreign income. When that effort failed, treaties were negotiated (but not ratified by the Senate) which would give a credit for taxes "spared" through foreign tax holidays. Other schemes were advanced to stimulate the outflow of private capital. In those days, a tax system based on strict principles of neutrality and equity seemed too restrictive.

Today the tide has turned. The Burke-Hartke bill would repeal the foreign tax credit, leaving only a deduction for taxes paid to foreign jurisdictions. Other less radical proposals would limit the extent to which foreign losses may be deducted against U.S. income, restrict the use of foreign corporate subsidiaries as a mechanism for deferring U.S. tax liability on retained earnings, and eliminate other preferences.[8] The argument is heard that U.S. firms have expanded abroad too rapidly, that jobs are being exported, that American technological leadership is threatened. In these days, a tax system based on neutrality and equity is seen as too generous.

Whatever the merits of these shifting contentions, the functional tax approach contains two inherent difficulties. The first difficulty is that goals may change more rapidly than the tax law. We are all familiar with the lags of diagnosis and response in applying monetary and fiscal policy: by the time the medicine is administered and takes effect, the fever has gone and the patient ends up with a chill. Functional taxation can encourage similar maladies. The tax code is littered with promotional schemes of past eras which have outlived their usefulness. In the international area alone we can point to several: the Western Hemisphere Trade Corporation, the preferential taxation of shipping income, the Domestic International Sales Corporation, and that little-known relic of the past, the China Trade Corporation. It may be hard to push a new tax preference through Congress, but it is far harder to repeal an old tax incentive. Once the tax law creates a vested-interest group, new arguments can always be found for old schemes.

The second difficulty with functional taxation is that it implies "tax expenditures" often hidden from public view. Professor Stanley Surrey argues that tax expenditures seldom receive the regular Congressional and Administrative scrutiny awarded to overt subsidy programs.[9] Certainly this is true of departures from neutrality and equity in the taxation of international income—departures which cost some $3.2 billion in 1974. Only a handful of tax lawyers and Washington bureaucrats understand the intricacies of these measures.

Despite these difficulties, I think we will increasingly see the use of functional taxation, not only in the international arena, but in all aspects of the revenue system. Neutrality and equity will continue to be observed in the liturgy of tax proposals, but not in the practicalities of legislation. To a conservative economist, this may not seem the best of all possible arrangements, but it is far better than direct government control of investment decisions, wages, and prices. Functional taxation has the great virtue of automatic administration. If the taxpayer is entitled to benefits, they are claimed on his return. No bureaucratic army is needed to choose between applicants or ponder economic decisions.

If the United States makes increasing use of functional taxation, the difficulties mentioned earlier must be addressed. The tax structure will have to respond more quickly to the changing needs of society. In an era of functional taxation we can no longer tolerate the view that preferences embedded in the Code might just as well be embedded in concrete. Moreover, Congressional and Administrative scrutiny of tax expenditures must be improved. The House Ways and Means Committee, now expanded to thirty-seven members, cannot be expected to evaluate the array of functional tax schemes proposed each session. Nor does the seventeen-member Senate Committee on Finance have the time or resources to assess these measures. Tax preferences also should be reviewed by other Congressional committees. Likewise, the Executive Branch should devote greater effort to the analysis of functional tax programs.

What functional goals make sense for international tax policy in the years ahead? I would suggest two.[10] With the rapid rise in the price of oil and other fuels, the United States will increasingly need to substitute capital for energy. This use of capital will come in addition to existing demands. Under these circumstances, I question whether the United States will want to provide substantial quantities of capital for the rest of the world. On this count, a more restrictive attitude towards the outflow of capital seems warranted. Indeed, as a first goal, the United States might modify its tax system to encourage a greater inflow of foreign capital.

Second, it might be useful if multinational firms were encouraged to invite greater participation by local investors. Local participation would ease nationalistic tensions. It would reduce the incentive for artificially high or low transfer prices, and it might diminish the pressure on U.S. capital markets. The U.S. tax law could be changed in certain obvious ways to promote local equity participation.

Protection

For many years the U.S. government has attempted to protect its citizens and corporations when they make investments beyond the frontier. The seizures associated with the Russian Revolution engaged public attention after the First World War. The United States later entered a protracted dispute with Mexico over the nationalization of petroleum and mineral resources. Since the Second World War, the U.S. government has attempted to mitigate the consequences of expropriation in Argentina, Ceylon, Chile, Peru, and numerous other countries.

The legal debate

U.S. government participation in foreign investment disputes may be defended or attacked on legalistic grounds. Since ancient times, a major purpose of diplomacy has been protection of the lives and property of citizens abroad. In legal terms, a corporation is endowed with many of the rights and immunities of an individual citizen. It is therefore argued that the foreign property of a U.S. corporation is entitled to the same diplomatic protection as that given any citizen abroad.

The legalistic approach can be debated either way. It could be pointed out that U.S. parent corporations often spawn foreign corporate subsidiaries as a vehicle for doing business abroad. A foreign corporation is a creation of foreign law. Just as the United States recognizes no duty to protect a foreign citizen, even if his parents happen to be American citizens, it might be suggested that the United States harbors no obligation to protect a foreign corporation, even if its parent happens to be an American corporation. Consistent with this position is the Latin American view, expressed in the Calvo doctrine, that the property rights of foreigners can only be protected and adjudicated in local courts. Yet, the United States would ordinarily look after the home or furnishings of an American citizen abroad. By the same token, the United States perhaps has an obligation to watch over the foreign holdings of a U.S. corporation, including its holdings of corporate shares.

The U.S. government frequently becomes involved at the borders of negotiation before it takes over a claim. In a very few cases, a treaty of friendship, commerce, and navigation, or a treaty of amity and economic relations will govern the course of negotiations. Generally, these treaties provide for just and prompt compensation, and the submission of disputes to the International Court of Justice. Since World War II, the United States has concluded only thirteen bilateral treaties with less developed nations. In more cases, an Overseas Private Investment Corporation bilateral treaty comes into play. These treaties, signed with about ninety countries, generally provide for binding arbitration. Finally, when a dispute arises with a nontreaty country, the U.S. government must fall back on its view of international law. Within European and the U.S. legal tradition, any taking may be judged improper which is not for a public purpose, is discriminatory, or where no provision is made for prompt, adequate, and effective compensation. According to the traditional view, compensation distinguishes expropriation from confiscation. Expropriation with compensation is a lawful act; expropriation without compensation is not.

Apart from diplomatic representation, the U.S. executive and judicial branches of government are seemingly compelled by legislation to take certain measures in response to expropriation. The Hickenlooper Amendment of 1962 requires suspension of assistance to any country which expropriates U.S. property and fails to take steps for adequate compensation within six months, unless the President determines that suspension would not be in the national interest. An amendment was added to the Sugar Act in 1962 which requires suspension of a country's sugar quota if it expropriates U.S. property without compensation. The Sabbatino amendment of 1964 prevents U.S. courts from declining to rule on the merits of a title claim arising out of an expropriation case. Thus, the erstwhile owner of an expropriated plant may sue for title to exports produced by the plant and shipped to the United States. In 1968, the Fisherman's Protective Act was amended to require that the Secretary of State withhold from foreign aid disbursements the amount of unpaid claims arising from the seizure of U.S. fishing vessels. In 1971, a similar article was applied to sales of military equipment. The Gonzales Amendment of 1972 instructs U.S. delegates to the various international development banks to vote against loans to any country which has expropriated property without provision for compensation. Finally, the Trade Act of 1974 would withhold the generalized system of preferences from any country which has expropriated U.S. property without provision for compensation or good-faith negotiations.

Diplomatic practice

These legalisms are interesting to pursue. Lawyers even regard them as decisive. But legalistic arguments overlook a fundamental feature of diplomacy. The essence of diplomacy is discretion. Despite the many instances of expropriation around the world, the United States has never invoked the full range of available sanctions. The congressional bark is a good deal fiercer than the executive bite.[11]

The practical question comes down to this: How vigorously should the United States protect the foreign economic interests of multinational enterprise? Should it content itself with polite protests? Should it cease economic aid and military assistance? Should it work to withhold International Monetary Fund, World Bank, and Regional Development Bank assistance? Should it break-off trade with the offending nation? A diplomatic effort of any substance must serve the national interest. The United States can hardly deploy its diplomatic artillery for every passing cause.

The first, and possibly most urgent, consideration is the domestic economic impact of foreign expropriation. The shares of multinational firms are widely held within the United States, not only by individuals, but also by pension funds, universities, and foundations. The losses of corporations and shareholders are partly shifted to the rest of the citizenry through the operation of the tax laws.[12] Other citizens must pay higher taxes to the Treasury when those directly affected pay lower taxes. Perhaps the tax laws should be amended so that investors themselves absorb a greater portion of the prospective costs entailed by foreign economic hostility. Diplomatic action is also costly. Retaliatory trade and investment measures impose hidden charges on the American public, and they affect the whole tenor of our relationship with foreign states.

A second consideration that shapes the appropriate response to expropriation is the United States' concern over the lines of supply. This concern centers on natural resources: petroleum, tin, copper, and certain other materials. The bulk of multinational investment, however, is lodged in manufacturing and service companies designed to supply the local market. At the end of 1973, the book value of such ventures was $70 billion, while the book value of all mining, smelting, and petroleum investments was $37 billion.

Both defenders of multinational enterprise and critics of the so-called imperialistic world order see a link between overseas investment and the supply of raw materials. But there is no assurance that security of investment can be equated with security of supply. Historically, mining and plantation ventures were inspired by the prospect of exporting to the U.S. market. Historically, host governments did not interfere with export shipments. But historical relationships do not govern present behavior. The lessons of OPEC (Organization of Petroleum Exporting Countries) are not lost on even the most obtuse Washington bureaucrat. Host governments are quite capable of interrupting exports, whether or not the resource is extracted by an American firm. In addition, the American multinational corporation has obligations to many importing countries, not solely or even primarily to the United States.[13]

A third consideration that affects the vigor of U.S. diplomacy is concern over the progress of less developed nations. The United States believes that a private enterprise market system holds great hope for economic progress. Multinational firms are seen as an agency for spreading private enterprise and improving the workings of a market economy. I share the belief that private enterprise can usefully promote economic development. But it seems to me that a market system must flower from local roots. To thrive, private enterprise requires a vigorous entrepreneurial and property-owning class. When companies are owned and controlled from abroad, this class may be stifled. Local hostility often blooms with the growth of multinational ownership. The countries which have conspicuously nationalized multinational corporations during the twentieth century—Mexico, Cuba, and Chile—stand out for an abundance of foreign investment, not a lack of it.[14]

Multinational enterprise may contribute in an important way to local accumulation of capital, labor skills, and technology. The question facing the developing nation is whether to kill the golden goose or to wait patiently for the eggs. Host governments are often too quick with the hatchet. The United States may be genuinely concerned about such folly in the face of pressing development needs. But whether the U.S. government should expend diplomatic effort protecting foreign countries from their own mistakes is an entirely different question.

Notes

Although the author is director of the International Tax Staff, U.S. Treasury, this paper does not necessarily reflect the views of the Treasury.

1. In addition, equity is often linked with the "ability to pay" doctrine.

2. A fuller treatment of this matter appears in G.C. Hufbauer, "U.S. Taxation of American Enterprise Abroad," unpublished manuscript, December 1974. The Senate version of the Tax Reduction Act of 1975 would have taxed foreign oil income in accordance with the principles of national neutrality.

3. The national neutrality approach might of course invite foreign retaliation.

4. In theory it might be advantageous to tax technology income earned abroad under a different system than capital income. In practice, any distinction would encourage the use of artificial transfer prices and create severe administrative problems.

5. When foreign taxes *exceed* the tentative U.S. tax on foreign source income, the excess foreign tax credit cannot be applied against the firm's tax liability on U.S. source income. Without this limit, the Treasury doors would be wide open to foreign governments. Likewise, foreign corporate subsidiaries cannot offset their losses against the parent firm's U.S. income. Nor is the investment tax credit or rapid depreciation under the asset depreciation range available for capital expenditures abroad. These various measures shield the Treasury at the sacrifice of pure capital-export neutrality.

6. The income of tax-haven enterprises may be taxed currently under the provisions of Subpart F. Subpart F was strengthened by the Tax Reduction Act of 1975.

7. Though, as I have tried to show, tax neutrality can be defined in different ways to achieve alternative welfare goals.

8. Some of these proposals are reflected in the Tax Reduction Act of 1975.

9. Stanley S. Surrey, *Pathways to Tax Reform: The Concept of Tax Expenditures* (Cambridge, Mass.: Harvard University Press, 1973).

10. To a limited extent, both these goals are reflected in the Tax Reduction Act of 1975.

11. Jessica Pernitz Einhorn, *Expropriation Politics* (Lexington, Mass.: D.C. Heath, 1974).

12. G.C. Hufbauer and P.H. Brigg, "Expropriation Losses and Tax Policy," Harvard International Law Journal 16 (Summer 1975): 533-64.

13. The multinational corporation can still play a role in improving U.S. lines of supply. Multinational firms might be encouraged to develop mines, oil fields, and plantations in many different countries, thereby weakening potential cartels. The United States might follow the Japanese style of *promoting* selected ventures without necessarily *protecting* the investment against nationalistic incursions.

14. The nationalized multinational firm is seldom returned to the private sector. The nationalizations of petroleum in Mexico, sugar and other enterprises in Cuba, tin in Bolivia, copper and petroleum in the Middle East have all resulted in the growth of state enterprise.

MULTINATIONAL CORPORATIONS AND TECHNOLOGY TRANSFER: THE NEED FOR A FRESH LOOK

GERHARD ROSEGGER

Events of the last quarter century have not dealt kindly with the traditional theory of international trade and investment. A number of reasons for this state of affairs can be adduced. Some, no doubt, simply reflect our reluctance to abandon well-entrenched textbook versions of accepted doctrine, especially once we have elaborated these into the logically elegant and intellectually challenging models with which we test our students' mettle. Intellectual historians may some day ponder why international economics – which by its very nature clearly belongs to the genus, *political* economy – was raised to the highest level of pure abstraction.

More important, however, are those reasons which explain the general tendency of political and institutional changes in the real world to outrun the capacity of economists – or, for that matter, of any other group of social scientists – to absorb new information, to digest it, and to reformulate their fundamental questions in light of new facts. It does not seem an unduly harsh judgment to say that the mainstream of neoclassical trade theory has run its traditional course, with only minor ripples and disturbances created by those phenomena which are difficult to accommodate in the context of that theory.

In recent years a number of findings have raised increasingly serious questions about the adequacy of accepted doctrine in explaining the observed patterns of trade and investment. We cannot possibly deal with all aspects of this challenge, but let me mention just a few examples. According to theory, the international flow of goods, services, and investment can be accounted for primarily by country-to-country differences in factor proportions, i.e., by each economy's endowment with capital per worker. But it was found that actual flows did not necessarily conform to the idea that a country's exports would consist of those goods produced with the help of its (relatively) most abundant, and therefore presumably cheapest, factor of production.[1] Furthermore, productivity growth and *changing* patterns of trade could not be explained by differing rates of change in countries' factor proportions. Finally, and perhaps most disconcertingly, international movements of capital did not necessarily go toward those countries where the productivity of capital would have been highest by the usual criteria; instead, the bulk of recent investment flows has led to a thorough intermeshing of the industrial machineries of developed, capital-rich nations.[2]

Efforts to absorb such findings into the existing corpus of theory cannot be said to have been resoundingly successful. On the other hand, an increasing number of investigations have shown that considerable explanatory power can be gained from a recognition of two phenomena largely ignored, or assumed out of the way, by conventional wisdom: the dynamic role played by technical innovations and their diffusion,[3] and the rapid growth of firms that seem to defy many of the orthodox tenets about trade and investment – the multinational corporations.

Thus, the last decade has seen not only a growing public concern with some of the implications of multinational business, but also a flood of academic writings about this new form of business organization.[4] At the same time, other writers began to chisel away at traditional theory's assumption that new technological knowledge is a free good that becomes available instantaneously to all firms and consumers.[5]

I think it is fair to say that the reaction on multinationals has been mixed. There is an inherent tendency to be suspicious of bigness, to worry about exploitation (whatever that term may be taken to mean), to explain the behavior of these firms by talking about their power rather than about the laws of the market place,[6] and to place them in juxtaposition to the sacred rights of the sovereign state.

Although an examination of these issues would far transcend my present charge, I cannot resist the temptation to comment on at least one aspect of the concern about multinationals – to wit, that their unquestioned economic success derives primarily from virtually unlimited exercises of power, economic *and* political. It seems to me that some of the so-called resource crises of recent years as well as a number of expropriations by host governments should have convinced us of the limits of political power. I am reasonably certain that such multinational giants as General Motors, Volkswagen, or Xerox, among many, wish right now that they could exercise some of their vaunted economic power to turn on international markets!

But on to my topic—the role of multinational corporations as agents of technological change. My thesis can be stated quite briefly: To explain developments in post–World War II trade and investment patterns one has to look to technological factors, in the broad sense. Key among these has been the rapid international diffusion of technology, and multinational firms have been the most important, and most successful, instruments for effecting diffusion. In this sense, the growth of multinationals represents the (at least temporary) culmination of a trend that was initiated by U.S. policy after the world war.

I propose to deal with these contentions by first examining what is meant by a transfer of technology and what conditions are necessary for its success. Then, on the basis of some limited historical evidence, I will trace the role of the United States in the international transfer of technology over the past quarter century in order to show that multinationals have indeed played a key role as agents of technological change. Finally I want to speculate on whether this particular phase in international economic development is not already beyond its peak growth and causing new patterns to emerge.

Transfer of Technology

Invention, innovation, and the rapid diffusion of innovations are generally regarded as socially desirable activities, despite current attacks by those who believe that the externalities resulting from further technological change are too high a price to pay at our present stage of development, and who therefore argue for some sort of "no-growth economy."[7]

The importance of technological advances to the solution of many of our present-day problems can be argued on several grounds: (1) the desperate need for further improvements in food production and food processing; (2) the need for accommodation of our productive capacity to changing availability of resources, not just in the energy field, but across a range of crucial raw materials; (3) the need to protect our ecological system; and (4) the widely accepted belief that any redistribution of real wealth between the "haves" and the "have-nots" of the globe is more likely to be effected in an expanding, than in a stagnating world economy.

Technology is not a *deus ex machina* which will solve these problems automatically, but it certainly forms an important component of solutions — expecially if we include under the rubric of technology those managerial and organizational innovations required to make our economic processes more efficient.[8]

But even if these arguments, which to me seem reasonably persuasive, were no longer to apply to the U.S. economy of the 1970s, there remains an incontrovertible fact: The rest of the world, both the industrialized and the developing nations, sees technological advancement as *the* key to further growth, is clamoring for more, and — with a few notable exceptions – brushes aside most of those reservations about social, economic, and cultural consequences that have begun to influence our thinking and our policies. In this connection I deliberately speak of the entire "rest of the world," for there exists little distinction between the technological aspirations of market economies and of socialist, or centrally planned, countries – or between the imperatives these aspirations impose on societies.[9]

For better or for worse, the United States has served as a model for what can be achieved with modern technology. Recent European concerns about a "technology gap," as well as the developing countries' refusal to be fobbed off with anything but the most up-to-date products and techniques, remind us of this country's unique position during the last few decades. This position has been one of provider of a wide range of technological knowledge to the rest of the world, either because of the United States' absolute leadership (mainly in a variety of so-called high-technology fields) or because of its seemingly greater ability to adapt and develop innovations made elsewhere, in order to make them suitable for large-scale, low-cost production.

I shall return to the reasons for this country's leadership later. Right now, I want to address another important question: How is technology transferred from one country to another?

Like so many concepts that have become part of casual sloganeering, "technology transfer" has come to mean many different things. Perhaps most misleading has been the idea that it is synonymous with "transmission of information." Given the rapid increase in the quantity and quality of our means of communication, some people have been led to believe that technology transfer has automatically increased at the same rate. But technology is not just useful knowledge, it is *used* knowledge. The mere transmission of technological information which is not utilized in production or consumption does not constitute diffusion in an economically meaningful sense.[10]

Thus, for our purposes, the transmission of information is a necessary, but not a sufficient, condition for technology transfer. From the following list of modes of transfer, it will become clear that, in some cases, utilization follows automatically as a consequence of transmission, whereas in others, information only is transferred. Clearly, we would expect different consequences to flow from these different modes, and with differing time lags. Consider the list:[11]

1. Some technical, and most scientific, knowledge is in the nature of a free good, i.e., it is available to all who wish to acquire it. Essential as such knowledge may be as part of the infrastructure of a modern economy, it has no *direct* consequences with respect to production or consumption.

2. Transfers can take place through the movement of people who

have special expertise in a technical field. How rapidly such expertise will be translated into productive results in the recipient country depends on a great variety of circumstances. Contrast, for example, the probability of success in the case of a consultant who has been invited to solve a specific technical problem in a specific plant and in the case of an expert who is trying to bring some new techniques of birth control to a country.

3. Proprietary technological knowledge can be sold like any other piece of property. In this case, the grant of a patent license (the most obvious example) will involve payments to the holder. At first glance, one would expect such economic obligations to act as a strong incentive for immediate utilization of the knowledge, but there is no assurance of this effect (see the story of the Wankel engine, for example).

4. Transfers may occur through the conscious imitation of another country's products. In some cases, such imitation may be relatively easy, which is of course why international patent protection is important to certain industries; in others, nontransferable know-how may have to be developed before imitation can be undertaken.

5. New technology may be embodied in capital equipment (or in whole plants) exported to another country. The effects of this type of transfer and the probability of its success will to some extent be influenced by the transactions underlying the transfer. It is useful to distinguish three different types of transaction:

a) Exports of capital goods to a purchaser in the recipient country. (It may even make a difference whether these exports are financed through normal commercial channels or whether they are the result of government-to-government grants or loans.)

b) Exports to establish a commercial joint venture between a firm in the exporting country and a firm in the recipient country.

c) Exports of equipment concomitant to the setting up of operations in the recipient country by a firm headquartered in the exporting country—i.e., direct investment.

As I intend to indicate later on, historical evidence suggests that there are indeed different impacts from these various modes of tranfer. The differences may of course be accentuated or weakened by other factors, prime among them the nature of the technology involved and the recipient country's capacity to absorb it.[12] I shall not deal with these in any detail.

One point, however, deserves emphasis in this connection: There has been much discussion about whether modern technologies are appropriate vehicles for the industrialization of developing countries. Issues raised have centered around differences in capital/labor ratios between developed and less developed economies and around the problem of market size versus minimum efficient scales for modern production techniques. It has often been assumed, at least by implication, that technological change in advanced countries has meant not only an automatic increase in the capital/labor ratio and increasing fixity of factor proportions, but also a similarly automatic rise in the minimum or optimal scales of operation. For at least three reasons, I think the importance of such considerations has been vastly exaggerated. First, there is considerable persuasiveness to the dynamic argument that a build-up of modern facilities is essential for sustained growth momentum, even if these facilities are out of step with the general economic environment. Second, empirical investigations have shown that many modern technologies are much less rigid in terms of factor proportions and scale than is frequently assumed in abstract discussions.[13] And third, even if neither of the first two points were true, there is still the simple political fact to which I have alluded earlier: less developed countries regard modern products and techniques as optimum launching pads for economic development and they are suspicious of all attempts to persuade them otherwise.

In other words, from the point of technology transfer, though not from other points of view, there is little need to distinguish between industrialized and developing countries. To state this is not to make light of tremendous differences in infrastructure, manpower availability, the socio-cultural setting, and so on, but to suggest that technology is one of the catalysts around which changes and adaptations of these other factors take place.[14] Nor can we ignore the fact that there has been a much greater lag in the diffusion of manufacturing technology to developing countries than in the diffusion of primary-producing techniques. But whenever diffusion does occur, there are few differences in the *quality* of technologies.

The Role of the United States and Its Multinational Corporations

Let us now place the problem of technology transfer into some historical perspective. For this purpose, it is useful to divide the period since World War II into three phases: (1) The era of government dominance and of the so-called dollar gap; (2) the period of heavy private capital flows and of the technology gap; and (3) the phase of convergence, with which I shall deal in the final section of this paper. My interest is not so much in delimiting these stages in a precise chronology, but in characterizing them with respect to the modes of technology transfer.

I call the first phase that of government dominance because it was largely in implementation of deliberate U.S. policy that transfers, or attempts at transfers, of technology took place. As several investigators have shown, a technology gap between the American economy and the rest of the world has existed for a long time.[15] This gap was accentuated by the war-time destruction of industrial capacity elsewhere in the world and by the growing aspirations of the less developed countries, many of whom were only just gaining political independence.

President Truman, in his inaugural address of 1949, expressed the desire of the United States to "make available to peace-loving people the benefits of our store of technical knowledge..."[16] Soon "productivity teams" scurried back and forth across the Atlantic, studying American production and marketing methods *in situ* or making suggestions to European managers and engineers. Meanwhile, our Point Four Program was to bring the benefits of modern technology to the developing world; indeed, technology was regarded as the touchstone for what would later be called the "take-off into development."

In other words, primary reliance was placed on making available "free-good knowledge" (through such activities as education and training programs) and on the exchange of people as means for transferring technology. The spectacular success of European industrial recovery probably reinforced belief in the efficacy of this policy, although the recovery probably owed more to the massive injections of Marshall Plan funds than to any technological miracles.

In the less developed world little happened as a result of these attempts to transfer technology, except for some quite remarkable accomplishments in the control of endemic diseases and in some other areas of social concern. But in the face of widespread underemployment even these successes had no great effect on production or productivity. Transferring bits and pieces from our store of technical knowledge was not sufficient by itself, and with the wisdom of hindsight we may wonder why anyone ever thought it would be.

In any event, the United States increased its commitment to government-to-government programs of assistance, involving the transfer of both financial and physical capital. But these transfers to less developed countries created a new problem: The recipients had to engage in some sort of reasonably comprehensive economic planning in order to identify opportunities and set priorities for investment schemes. Whatever successes these schemes may have had, high technical and economic efficiency was generally not one of their characteristics.

As it turned out, the questionable record of these undertakings simply served to reinforce our policy-makers' ideological predispositions, which clearly lay in the direction of a reliance on the marketplace rather than on planning as a determinant of investment opportunities. Not too surprisingly, it was President Eisenhower who gave strongest expression to these feelings, in 1955:

> The whole free world needs capital; America is its largest source. In that light, the flow of capital abroad from our country must be stimulated and in

such a manner that it results in investment largely by individuals or private enterprises rather than by government....[17]

Such pronouncements, even when they come from the President of the United States, do not signal an immediate retrenchment of policy...or conversion of two-thirds of the world to the virtues of free capital markets. But, whatever the lags and political and economic disagreements which may have accompanied it, a massive and rapid transfer of dollars *and* technology through private investment was now recognized as essential. This recognition was no doubt hastened by the widespread belief that the rest of the world was suffering from an acute "dollar shortage." Unfortunately, this belief also tended to obscure the essential differences between transfers of financial capital (with few or no direct technological consequences) and transfers of physical capital in connection with direct investment.

Thus it was not at all clear what institutional innovations would best implement the process of transfer. As late as 1960, an expert could judge that "...the United States has continued to seek *the* magic formula that might serve to unleash a flow of private capital of unprecedented magnitude toward foreign investment outlets,"[18] when in reality developments were already underway which we can now recognize as harbingers of precisely such a flow. Let me identify just a few of them: the so-called economic miracle of Western Europe, regional economic integration movements, the subsidence of the strident cold war into a more subdued form of political and economic competition, the emergence of Japan as a major economic power, and the rapid disintegration of the old colonial empires.

But the biggest changes probably occurred in the United States. Just as market capitalism may be said to have characterized the growth of nationwide corporations around the turn of the century and finance capitalism the boom of the 1920s, so the 1950s witnessed the emergence of what one is tempted to call technology capitalism. There is no need to enumerate here all the significant innovations in products and processes on the basis of which new markets were developed, new firms sprang up, and old firms grew in new directions. The shock of Sputnik and the subsequent heavy public investment in a scientific and technological competition with the Soviet Union—and, therefore, also in education—hastened all these changes.

These developments had two important consequences: (1) The lead of the United States in the so-called high technology fields and in mass-production techniques for new consumer goods continued and perhaps even lengthened; (2) American firms began to look intensively for outlets abroad, especially in those areas of the world where either natural resources or growing markets promised success beyond what could be achieved in the domestic economy.

Clearly, the exploitation of natural resources (minerals prime among them) required direct investment, with the attendant transfer of American equipment and technical knowledge, particularly since most of these resources were found in the less developed countries. But, even in the case of the burgeoning capital and consumer goods markets, setting up manufacturing operations abroad appeared more attractive than traditional exporting channels or the licensing of foreign firms. The attractions were many: easing the adaptation of products to local or regional requirements; avoiding tariff and nontariff barriers to trade; taking advantage of then generally lower labor costs; gaining access to foreign financing; providing necessary customer services; seeking the most favorable tax climate, etc.

The figures illustrating this development are well known: In 1955, U.S. direct investment abroad totalled $19.3 billion; by 1960, it had grown to $31.9 billion; and in 1970, to $78.1 billion. But, as I hope to show, the technological impact of the corporate rush into multinational operations went well beyond what can be measured by these statistics. In order to make this point, I ask two questions: What accounted for the technological lead of American firms in so many sectors? And why were they successful as technological transfer agents?

The literature on the reasons for the technology gap is extensive, and I do not propose to review it here. But I do want to comment briefly on a few matters. For example, much has been made of the United States' allegedly inherent superiority in basic science and in technical education. Similarly, our large expenditures for research and development have been credited with the success of our industries, as has been our ability to attract some of the finest technical minds from all over the world. No doubt, these and similar factors play a role in that success in the sense that they are part and parcel of our total technology system. But when we attempt to trace their linkages to specific technological events, the distinction between cause and effect quickly blurs.

Support for such contentions comes primarily from data gathered in the context of our government's huge expenditures for technological developments (through to final products) in defense, space, and nuclear energy. No doubt these activities contributed to our great technological adventures and provided ample employment for scientists and technologists and contributed heavily to the much-maligned brain drain. But we also know that expectations of substantial spill-overs or spin-offs from these undertakings into the private sector were vastly exaggerated with benefits accruing primarily to the aircraft, computer, and industrial electronics industries.

I am much more inclined to give credence to explanations of our technological leadership position which deal with the size of our home markets, with the structure of product and process competition in these markets, and with the high geographic and social mobility of the U.S. population. The story has been told too often to bear repeating. But even here I want to register some caveats.

First, it is assumed too often that the scale economies which result from our firms' access to a large home market are in some sense separable from technological factors. But large-scale production systems are not simply blown-up versions of small-scale. Each level of scale in a given industry requires its own unique technological adjustments, degrees of specialization, and composition of output. Thus, scale changes and technological changes are inextricable.

Second, the attribution of some separate identity to scale as such has frequently misled us into an unwarranted exaggeration of the role of corporate giants in the creation of new technology. The reasoning seems to go like this: Modern innovations require a carefully planned and organized research and development effort; the more a firm spends on research and development (R & D), the more likely it is to come up with important innovations; large firms spend (absolutely) more on R & D than small ones – ergo, the giants are the key to technical progress.

Unfortunately, things are not quite that simple, and the fact that the same examples always seem to be used to support this kind of reasoning should make us suspicious. These examples typically include missiles, aircraft, and computers – all of which relied heavily on government funding for development. We have ample evidence that small and medium-size firms play an extremely important role in the advancement of civilian technology. Even more significantly, there exists only tenuous evidence at best that the number or significance of innovations is in any way related to expenditures on R & D. Here again, it is all too easy to assume that because this linkage existed in some cases of spectacular technological undertakings, it can be generalized to the whole economy.[19]

Third, I would propose that the dynamic effects of innovations in products and processes, with the entry of new firms into the territories of seemingly well-entrenched giants, and with the abandonment of whole product lines by these giants, suggests the need for re-examination even of the thesis that it is only the technological rivalry of large, oligopolistic firms which stimulates their branching out into multinational operations.[20]

Thus, I would suspect that the technological advantages of American firms were not restricted to the huge corporations but were probably more deeply rooted in a range of economic, technical, and social features of our system. Among these, I would certainly list what is generally regarded as a greater flexibility, especially of the managements of small and medium-size firms, in responding to technological and market challenges.[21]

There are of course great difficulties in supporting such assertions. In our efforts at empirical verification, we are by the very nature of the problem (and by the availability of data) attracted to the big, spectacular innovations and to the big, spectacular success stories . . .or failures. Therefore, I think honesty compels us to say that the reasons for the ''technology gap'' are somewhat unclear.

My second question, which is why multinational firms are such successful agents in the transfer of technology, is probably somewhat easier to answer. I contend that their achievements in this respect rest on their ability to combine in a purposeful manner all the various modes of technology transfer which I listed earlier. To be sure, transfer in the narrower sense occurred through direct investment in plants and facilities, but this was only the tip of the iceberg. However wrong he may have been about other aspects of the ''American challenge,''[22] the alarmist M. Servan-Schreiber was right on the track in his very broad (one is tempted to say, humanistic) assessment of the technological impact of multinationals on their host countries. Thus I believe that the Americanization of business around these outposts, about which so many foreign politicians and writers complained, was not just a product of their imaginations. Rather, it reflected in the managerial and technological context something akin to the ''Coca-Cola culture'' with which American military establishments abroad quickly surrounded themselves.

Convergence . . . and Second Thoughts

What should rightly follow here is a diagnosis of the effects of multinationals on the structure of U.S. trade and on the balance of payments, but this would clearly go beyond our present scope. Similarly, we have omitted any consideration of the role of foreign multinationals in the exchange of technology; it is no doubt significant and growing. In the period I am talking about, however, the late fifties and sixties, technology transfer was mainly a one-way street. This observation is substantiated by the fact that, even in just the measurable portion of transfer, among the eight countries with the highest per capita output only the United States had a surplus on its technological balance-of-payments account.[23]

Looking at the growth of American and foreign multinationals over the last two decades, and using the methods of computerized extrapolation now popular in some quarters, we could no doubt show that by the year 2000 all the world's real assets will be owned by these new social inventions. But by using a historical perspective, as I have tried to do, we may be able to claim that the heyday of multinationals as agents in the rapid leveling of technology around the globe is already past.

In this perspective, the fifties and sixties can be considered as a period of convergence among economies with respect to patterns of production. To be sure, there are substantial lags in this process of convergence, especially in those areas of the world where poverty or the maldistribution of incomes has prevented any pervasive spread of modern technologies, but what technologies we find there are not uniquely different, if they have been imported recently. Similarly, the emergence of a consumer-oriented economic structure in the Soviet Bloc has been slow, but the direction of change seems clear.

Two major factors appear responsible for this on-going convergence. The first, which I shall mention only briefly, is of course the radical change in our government's policies with respect to private foreign investment which occurred in the 1960s. Concerns about our balance of payments, political responses to American labor's fears about having jobs exported, the difficulties of maintaining some sort of sovereign authority over multinational corporations, and a variety of diplomatic and strategic considerations, all no doubt contributed to the shift in our policy—from active encouragement to more or less benign neutrality, or even active discouragement of foreign investment.

A second set of factors, however, appears to me more important in producing this convergence. These factors are themselves effects of the very success of multinationals in transferring American technology and managerial styles to the rest of the world. This success, as I have suggested, must be gauged not only at the level of directly observable and measurable results reflected in specific economic indicators, but also at other, much less clearly defined levels concerned with the broader effects of imported technology on the economic and social systems of the host countries.

At the measurable level one turns of course to those indicators generally examined by economists: changes in per capita output, changes in income distribution, changes in the structure of output, changes in consumption patterns and in the composition of foreign trade, etc. Needless to say, such changes are not solely attributable to infusions of new technology and new managerial attitudes. They cannot be separated from the two other main effects of foreign investment—the absorption of resources which were previously idle, and the redirection of other resources from low-productivity to higher-productivity sectors of the host economy.

Even after allowing for difficulties of measurement, however, one may surely claim that there has been a measurable and remarkable degree of technological convergence among the "older" industrial economies, and a strong tendency in the same direction among other countries.

When all is said and done, formal measures are slightly dissatisfying.

For it seems to me that the real impact of the multinationals' so-called success goes far beyond quantifiable effects. I have used such vague concepts as the American technological system, managerial styles, and the Americanization of foreign economies. Ill-defined as these concepts may be, they nevertheless refer to very real phenomena.

At the most general level, Kenneth Boulding has very aptly described the development of what he calls a technology-induced superculture, which frequently lives in tension with the more traditional cultural systems on which it is an overlay.[24] He deals with the question of whether technology's challenges to traditional values will lead to accommodation or disintegration, and his answer is wisely tentative.

But I think that somewhere between hard statistics and the broadly cultural contemplation of technology transfer there is an intermediate level of analysis which deals with the specific reactions and adaptations of host economies to importation of new technologies and new managerial-organizational forms. Let me offer just a few examples:

1. There can be little doubt that the well-known "demonstration effect" has elicited responsive innovations from multinational corporations' suppliers and customers abroad. Competition saw to that.

2. It is more frequently asserted that the technological standard of foreign economies has caught up with the international level or with leading industrial sectors in other countries. Such statements are not as speculative as they appear. At any given time, the technological standard of an established industry will reflect the extent to which leading, average, and marginal techniques of production are embodied in its plants. The relevant measure of convergence clearly is what happens to the average and not whether a few showpiece plants represent the most modern technology. I think one may safely claim that, in this sense, multinational firms have served to hasten the raising of the technological standard.

3. The success of technology-based multinational firms has stimulated many host economies to re-allocate resources toward more research and development. Indeed, discussions of how science policy and R & D policy might enhance the development of indigenous technology have become commonplace around the world. It is not at all clear that countries will indeed gain from such a re-allocation. At this point considerations of national prestige, etc., begin to clash with potential comparative advantages in the development of technology. The checkered histories of computer and commercial aircraft production in Western Europe serve as fine illustrations of the problem.

4. Foreign manufacturers have adapted many American high technologies and mass-production techniques to the unique requirements of their own markets and have thus been able to prevail over the competition of United States companies. Whether such changes conform

to some general product life cycle pattern in the international division of labor remains an open question.[25]

5. American techniques in production logistics and marketing have been diffused much more rapidly than any statistics on overseas operations suggest. The interest in these techniques has of course helped many U.S. consulting firms join the ranks of multinational enterprise.

We could extend this list of intermediate-level effects, but I think the point is made: Convergence is not a measurable state, but an on-going *process,* which has marked the directions technological effort has taken around the globe. This process has been hastened significantly by the role of multinational corporations as agents of the transfer of technology.

There is no better evidence for the success of the process than the appearance of a body of revisionist thought during the last few years.[26] According to this interpretation of events, the technology gap was vastly exaggerated; Europe and Japan had in fact always enjoyed a lead in "low-technology" products; multinationals, because of their monopoly position in many markets, often retarded rather than advanced technological progress; American preoccupation with a narrow range of industries has diverted attention from many private sectors in which technological change has actually been slow. In other words, the American challenge was a sham.

While such pronouncements may serve as a useful antidote to overly exuberant technological flag-waving on our part, I do believe they fail in historical perspective. I suspect very strongly that, with the wisdom of considerably more hindsight, we shall come to regard the past quarter century not only as one of momentous technological advancement, especially in the United States, but also as one of a remarkable spread of new products and techniques around the globe, a spread which was instrumentally fostered by multinational business.

Whether we applaud or deplore the broader effects of technological change on our social institutions and on the quality of our lives, a fresh look at the role of multinational corporations should at least bring home one truth which is too often forgotten – technology is not an autonomous force; it interacts in manifold and complicated ways with our society and our values. Ultimately, to harness technology means to innovate in the ways in which we manage the total range of our human affairs.

Notes

NOTE: The author is grateful to his colleague Asim Erdilek for many thoughtful comments on an earlier version of this paper.

1. The Leontief Paradox has in fact found its way even into many basic textbooks, although efforts to accommodate it are typically still in the strictly neoclassical tradition.

2. For a comprehensive discussion of these issues, see R.R. Nelson, M.J. Peck, and E.D. Kalachek, *Technology, Economic Growth, and Public Policy* (Washington, D.C.: The Brookings Institution, 1967).

3. These innovations include not only technological changes in the narrower sense, but also organizational and managerial changes.

4. Even a partial listing of this literature is impossible; however, a good impression of the scope of work can be gained from C.P. Kindleberger, ed., *The International Corporation* (Cambridge, Mass.: M.I.T. Press, 1970), and from S. Lea and S. Webley, *Multinational Corporations in Developed Countries: A Review of Recent Research and Policy Thinking* (New York: British–North American Committee, 1973).

5. See, for example, R.R. Nelson and S.G. Winter, "Toward an Evolutionary Theory of Economic Capabilities," *American Economic Review,* Papers and Proceedings, 63, No. 2 (May 1973): 440-49.

6. The ambivalence of such efforts is illustrated by S. Hymer, "The Efficiency (Contradictions) of Multinational Corporations," *American Economic Review,* Papers and Proceedings, 60, No. 2 (May 1970): 441-48.

7. A selection of excellent papers on this subject, as well as a telling rebuttal to the absolute no-growth school, can be found in M. Olson and H.H. Landsberg, *The No-Growth Society* (New York: Norton, 1973).

8. Herbert Simon has argued for the importance of such innovations, which he refers to as meta-technology, in "Technology and Environment," *Management Science,* Application Series, 19, No. 10 (June 1973): 1110-21.

9. On this point, see R.L. Heilbroner, *An Inquiry into the Human Prospect* (New York: Norton, 1974), esp. chap. 3.

10. The argument is elaborated in G. Rosegger, "The Diffusion of Innovations in Industry: Some Conceptual Questions for Economic Research," Working Paper No. 57, Research Program in Industrial Economics, Case Western Reserve University (Dec. 1974).

11. A somewhat different taxonomy is presented by J.H. Dunning, "Technology, United States Investment, and European Economic Growth," in Kindleberger, *The International Corporation,* pp. 141-76, esp. 158ff.

12. These factors are dealt with in detail by J. Baranson, "Technology Transfer through the International Firm," *American Economic Review,* Papers and Proceedings, 60, No. 2 (May 1970): 435-40.

13. For an example from one industry, see G. Rosegger, "Scale Considerations in the Industrialization of Developing Countries: The Case of Steel," *I.T.C.C. Review,* Special Issue, 3d World Congress of Engineers and Architects, Tel Aviv, Jan. 1974, pp. 47-60.

14. The dynamic argument is made most persuasively by A. Zauberman, *Industrial Progress in Poland, Czechoslovakia,and East Germany, 1937-1962* (London: Oxford University Press, 1964); see especially chap. 1, "The Economic Mechanism and the Strategy of Industrial Growth."

15. *Cf.* R.R. Nelson, "The Technology Gap: Analysis and Appraisal," Clearinghouse for Federal Scientific and Technical Information, Dec. 1967 (mimeo.).

16. Cited in W. Krause, *Economic Development* (San Francisco: Wadsworth Publishing Co., 1961), p. 305.

17. *Ibid.*

18. *Ibid., p. 304.*

19. For a detailed critique of the conventional wisdom, see B. Gold, "The Framework of Decision for Major Technological Innovation," in *Values and the Future,* ed. by K. Baier and N. Rescher (New York: Free Press, 1969), pp. 389-430.

20. Interesting evidence on the role of smaller firms is presented by J.M. Roach, "The Mini-Multinationals," *The Conference Board Record,* Feb. 1974, pp. 27-31.

21. For a comprehensive survey of factors, see Organization for Economic Cooperation and Development, *The Conditions for Success in Technological Innovation* (Paris, France, 1971).

22. J.J. Servan-Schreiber, *Le Défi américain* (Paris France,: Editions de Noël, 1967).

23. Dunning, "Technology, U.S. Investment . . . Growth," 156.

24. K. Boulding, "The Emerging Superculture," in *Values and the Future,* pp. 336-50.

25. *Cf.*, S. Rose, "Multinational Corporations in a Tough New World," *Fortune* 88, No. 2 (Aug. 1973): 52ff.

26. These shifts in interpretation are discussed by H. Brooks, "Have the Circumstances that Placed the United States in the Lead in Science and Technology Changed?" in *Science Policy and Business,* ed. by D.W. Ewing (Cambridge, Mass.: Harvard University Press, 1973), pp. 11-32.

THE SCOPE FOR REVERSAL:
FOREIGN FIRMS IN THE U.S. ECONOMY

WILLIAM G. SHEPHERD

To round out this series, I will reverse the usual line of analysis of international corporations and consider whether foreign firms are likely to move into U.S. markets and what we might best do about it. After decades of U.S. moves outward, there are signs of a reversal. This might have a strong impact, one perhaps more effective than changes now likely to come from within.

The roots of the issue go very deep. Adam Smith, Stuart Mill, indeed all the classical and neo-classical greats, have assured us that free trade and interactions among large firms will remove monopoly and give good economic performance. To some—perhaps a large—extent this has actually occurred from U.S. firms acting abroad, seeking out gains that have not been realized by foreign firms, and applying competitive pressure.[1] That is the conventional rationale for U.S. multinational firms. Indeed the U.S. public assists them by various tax concessions. And even if there were no such competitive pressure, there is still the common belief abroad that it exists, often unfairly.

So far it has seemed to be a lopsided contest with the U.S. firms playing a dominant role. The natural question is, will the process also work in reverse? Will foreign firms move into the U.S. economy along similar lines and apply the same economic pressures, with the same effects? This question divides into several specific parts: Has it done so in the past? Will it do so in the future? In any case, what would be the proper policy response to it?

The last several years have made it clear that the potential for reversal is growing. Large, diverse, and powerful foreign firms have been in existence for a long time – since formation of the East India Company and even earlier – but there now appear to be new factors at work. One is Arabian oil money, but there are wider sources, also. In general, it seems reasonably clear that U.S. economic supremacy, to which we grew accustomed during the Augustan age of 1940-65, has peaked and is fading. We are now one among several major international competitive groupings. Many of our major industries are showing a new vulnerability to international rivals and incursions.

The kinds of new incursions and pressures into U.S. markets from abroad are much broader than just the direct ones of international firms. Unilever, Nestlé, Mitsui, and the other 100 largest, foreign-based, multinational firms are only part of the larger process of international trade and interaction. But they are likely to be a larger part of the process in the future, perhaps the most important part. The issue is at the frontier between the fields of international trade and industrial organization. Each study has been separate from the other in the past and has achieved much rigor and specific findings.[2] But separately they may miss the essential effects of large, diverse, international company operations.

In this paper I will first define several basic concepts. Then I will look backward at the trends in multinational firms since 1900. Next I will analyze the parts and conditions in the U.S. economy which might be especially subject to corrective forces from foreign multinational operations. Finally, I will take up some of the obvious policy questions, such as what, if anything, the United States should do about inward moves by foreign firms.

Basic Concepts

There are three ways in which foreign operations might affect U.S. markets. One is by extending *financial control* – by a shift in portfolio holdings, share holdings, or other partial or complete takeover operations. Perhaps a Middle Eastern, oil-rich emirate decides to take over a significant U.S. company and succeeds. Or, less colorfully, perhaps a diversified foreign company simply adds to its holdings, gaining partial or complete control of a firm located in the United States. This shift may take any number of forms and degrees, but it is financial control.

The second way of affecting U.S. markets is more concrete – It is the building by an international company of a *new productive capacity* in the United States which then increases the volume of domestic production. Recently there has been some such expansion, and further plans are reported. Individual U.S. states and cities have been competing to attract these plants.

The third way is by conventional *import* competition – goods made abroad and sold here.

All of these are routine parts of commercial and industrial operations both at home and abroad. They have all occurred in large measure from the United States outward.

U.S. firms abroad

The earlier lecturers in this series and many other analysts have explored the effects of these outward moves. The effects have not been trivial, and the U.S. firms include some very large industrial units. Table 1 lists some of the more prominent ones among its tentative listing of the leading dominant firms in U.S. industry. These firms have moved abroad extensively, with a variety of specific – and often important – effects on international markets and foreign national markets.

This outward flow has thrived during a very special era of conditions which have favored the big American firms. Thus, there are American multinationals with important positions in a wide range of British, European, and other markets. Their effects may have been of the classic sort one expects from a newcomer – new technology and competitive attitudes.

Part of this effect comes from increasing capacity, which has occurred in many markets. Second, the shift also has tended to reduce the degree of monopoly, either directly or merely by import competition. U.S. firms have often reduced the stability of the local cartel simply because newcomers from America often have not lived by the old rules.

Many U.S. multinationals have infused new technology and management methods in foreign markets. Although the American technological contribution may have been grossly exaggerated, the foreign reactions to the American "challenge" indicate some fear and some response, at the least. The old ways have been challenged and altered in some cases. If indeed U.S. firms excel at innovation and professional management, then perhaps these firms have been exporting good performance.

Perhaps less obviously beneficial has been the tendency of the American presence to dilute the sovereignty of countries abroad. (There has been genuine anguish among the British as parts of their choice industries have been bought out by Americans during the last several decades. The anguish may have been misdirected, but it has been real.) The acquisition of choice industries has left many nations with less sovereignty, with less domestic control over the essentials of their own economic activity. And in many small, developing countries the advent or presence of a sizable U.S. company has had larger effects. Sovereignty is one of those noneconomic concepts which may matter – at least socially – more than any of the others. It certainly is affected by international moves of capital and management. (Some of the previous lectures in the series have touched on these effects. I had hoped they would provide a complete catalog: they have covered more the impact on America caused by our firms' going abroad. Those effects are undoubtedly significant, but the full evaluation of what the American businesses have done to foreign markets remains to be written.) A U.S. corporation abroad is probably not fungible with other corporations. It may do things differently, with effects that are different.

The Larger Setting

Now consider the possible scope and effect of reversing this process. First we need to evaluate the setting within which the reversal might take place. During the 1870 to 1910 period, the investment flows were mainly from Europe to the United States. When we were a less developed country ourselves, we absorbed a lot of British capital for railroads and other industrial growth. A great deal of it was handled by the Morgans and other leading financial houses, so banking connections were important from the start. The flow of capital was complex and important, but it did not carry much direct control by the original foreign investors. This was partly because of the way the Morgans handled it and partly because of the way most British investors looked at the world. It was enough if they could count on good people managing their foreign assets in a reliable way. British investors were content not to go abroad themselves to create and manage industrial capacity. That was perhaps a glory of the British and also, perhaps, a failure. But in any case, investment was made mainly by relatively passive portfolio management rather than by branching out to other countries across the water by existing British firms. By 1900, despite the great volume of capital that had flowed into the United States, there were few significant international footholds in U.S. markets.

Then the tides shifted. Not long after the turn of the century substantial U.S. tariffs were established to limit free trade. At the same time the United States shifted towards investing abroad, rather than remaining a recipient country, and the moves outward by large U.S. companies into international markets grew.

Essentially there have been two waves in this flow since 1900. The early one stretched for a fairly long time, from about 1910 to 1940. By then U.S. companies had made important outward moves into more than portfolio holdings abroad. Instead of exporting goods into European markets, the United States was exporting management control and the ownership of capital. Procter & Gamble, Kodak, General Motors, and Ford made early entries into foreign markets. There were also some oil firms and meat packers. Sewing machines were a classic example of the flow. A variety of consumer oriented companies such as Heinz & Company were exporting American advertising techniques as well as manufacturing capability, all of which established a real U.S. presence in many markets by World War II.

Since the war there has been a further shift, differing to some extent because of the higher technology involved in many industries. This includes computers, an area where IBM may now have a stronger position internationally than it does in the United States. Drug companies now selling abroad are at a large scale; more oil companies are moving abroad; Gillette, Xerox, and Caterpillar Tractor are other obvious examples. Perhaps most interesting and important of all has been the United States foreign activities in banking during the last fifteen years, the importance of which will be noted later. These were no small shifts, and I have mentioned only a few of them. Many other sectors underwent very little shift, however, and there is no full explanation of the differences, industry by industry, although there is surely a large random element in each industry, including personalities, judgment, and historical accidents.

Certain industries have had relatively well-known international cartels that prevented competitive American firms from moving abroad aggressively. Electrical equipment is one such cartel. Book publishing is another; perhaps best-known was the chemicals cartel prior to World War II (which may indeed have affected the flow and duration of that great war). In the cigarette industry the division between American Tobacco and its British counterpart was made as early as the turn of the century. In such situations, U.S. firms have acquiesced in agreements which keep them at home.

The whole pattern therefore includes an important but incomplete set of moves outward by U.S. firms, which did not bring to every possible monopoly market abroad the benefits of new U.S. competition. This broad-scale move may have run its course, and the balance may be shifting. We now appear to be in a watershed period of many flows and moves. Some hypothesize that there has been a reactive process: whenever an American firm goes abroad into industry X there may be a reaction and European firms in industry X move into the United States in a form of stimulus and response. There are hints that this occurs on a short-run basis over a period of a few years.[3] But the longer-run patterns, which are our main concern, have been little studied. We do not know if a future process of shifts into U.S. markets would follow a systematic pattern. The research has not yet been done.

"Target Industries" in the United States

Recent research has helped to identify the most important industries having dominant firms in the U.S. economy. (See firms in Table 1.) Others are tight oligopolies with high entry barriers of one kind or another.[4] These are the counterparts of the industries American firms may have been moving into abroad, mopping up excess profits, energizing sluggish managements, increasing competition. If we are ripe for a reversal of multinational moves, these U.S. industries (grouped in Table 2) would presumably attract foreign incursions. Taking these as so-called target industries in the United States, we may now ask whether the shifts have already begun or are likely to happen. What may govern them? What is the best policy approach? It seems improbable that the market power in these U.S. industries will be briskly reduced either by antitrust policy or by natural erosion of market shares.[5] To this degree, moves inward by foreign firms may be particularly beneficial.

TABLE 1
Selected Dominant and Multinational Firms in the United States

Sales Rank, 1973	Firms	Percentage of Estimated Average Market Share in Its Primary Markets
8	*IBM	70
1	*General Motors	55
12	Western Electric	98
5	*General Electric	50
25	*Eastern Kodak	70
41	*Xerox	80
30	*Procter & Gamble	50
69	*Coca-Cola	50
59	United Aircraft	40
139	Campbell Soup	75
158	*Gillette	70
197	*Kellogg	45

Multinational Firms Not Dominant

*Exxon
*Ford
*Westinghouse
*Various drug firms
*RCA
*Caterpillar Tractor
*W.R. Grace
*Continental Can

*Denotes high involvement in foreign markets.
Sources: W.G. Shepherd, *The Treatment of Market Power* (New York: Columbia University Press, 1975), and various company and trade reports.

Actually, there have already been some strong moves inward, touching precisely on target industries. Two prominent instances are the automobile and steel industries, where an import share of as little as 15 percent gained by foreign firms has had a very strong effect. The same effect presumably would apply in other industries, too. Therefore, it appears that even relatively small inward movements can change competitive climate strongly. Note that these two cases have occurred even during the period of U.S. advantages. Many of the specific target industries in the United States may be quite sensitive to stress from international competitors, even if there is no tidal flow inward. Foreign-firm moves can substitute for domestic competition and thus do part of the Antitrust Division's work for it.

There are other sectors where some shift has recently occurred. Yet most of the problem still remains untouched. Most of the industries in Table 2 have had high market power for a long time, some for almost as long as a century. Most of them look as though they will be staying in roughly their present positions for a good time longer. They therefore can be regarded as needing treatment from some direction.[6]

Two types of industry

Foreign firms may be the best hope, via the three kinds of inward movement. How can we distinguish where they may have an effect? I would begin by dividing the target industries into two kinds of sectors

TABLE 2

Principal Target Industries in the United States

Hard	*Soft*
Computers	Automobiles
Telecommunication equipment	Iron and steel
Heavy electrical equipment	Glass
Photographic supplies	Nonferrous metals
Copying equipment	Banking
Detergents	Airlines
Soaps	Tires and tubes
Earth-moving equipment	Meatpacking
Newspapers	Electrical appliances
Drugs	
Razor blades, toiletries	
Aircraft and engines	

and calling them soft and hard industries. The labels are inexact, but the meaning is reasonably apparent. Consider the industries in each category. IBM is a good example of a so-called hard competitor. It is aggressive; it has moved outward already; it can easily resist incursions. By contrast, steel and automobiles have become soft industries during the last fifteen years. The glass and metals industries have been relatively soft for a variety of reasons. U.S. banking has been rather soft, though some leading banks have become more aggressive since 1965. I invite you to evaluate the industries yourself, to determine which of the target industries are relatively vulnerable to international competition, or perhaps to international take-over. By contrast, hard industries would include IBM, Procter & Gamble, Eastman Kodak, many of the drug companies, Coca-Cola, Xerox, Gillette, Caterpillar Tractor, and Western Electric. These are industries where the dominant firm is strong, lucrative, long-established, and likely to resist strongly or retaliate against incursions. Note that oligopolies tend to be soft while dominant firm industries are mostly hard.

One of the reasons for the difference between soft and hard relates to banking. Consider briefly the basic banking relationship. Usually there is a single main banker to which the company has been going for short-term capital (and more recently its long-term capital) for, perhaps, decades, often since it was founded. The banking relationship is basically between the chief financial officers of the company and a senior loan official or vice president of this bank. This relationship is important because it influences what the company can do. It determines the degree of support the company can expect in its ventures and the extent of support the company will have if attacked. Indeed in many markets the competitive struggle between existing companies or between established firms and a newcomer is essentially a conflict between the banks backing these companies. (In the 1960s a good deal of the conglomerate merger phenomenon was the sum total of a few relatively small-scale operators who persuaded certain banks to break ranks and back outsiders.)

The banking relationship is often a primary factor in trying to understand why a company does what it does and what it can be expected to do in the future. A company without primary backing from a good solid bank simply does not have the competitive force it would have with a strong banking relationship. Therefore, it is important to include the roles of bankers in thinking about domestic competition and the target industries. It is especially important to think about this in appraising prospects for international moves. To some extent the inward moves of foreign firms are likely to be governed by the relative strength of the bankers of American companies and the bankers of foreign ones. If the bankers of the foreign companies do not have the staying power or strong interest necessary to get into U.S. markets or to take over U.S.

firms, that may be the decisive factor in the success or failure of the move.

Multinational companies, even the largest ones, may simply be manufacturing enterprises lacking sufficient bank backing. Most companies don't go it alone, and those that do – e.g., drug companies – are often in the industries where their U.S. adversaries are unusually well financed. In the 1950s a lot of U.S. companies were able to generate sufficient cash flows to be independent of outside finance. In the last 15 years, however, banks have made a major shift toward long-term lending to companies. Consequently, in many companies the banking relationship has become closer and more controlling. The bank, as adviser and as supplier of capital, is often almost a part of the company.

In many cases bank controls are even tighter for European firms, where banking relationships have traditionally been more intimate and thorough. Often the bank owns stock in the company. Its officials mingle, more or less informally, with the roles taken by company officials. That has also been true in Japan, in the earlier Zaibatsu combines, and also more recently (although after World War II Allied trustbusting caused some marginal reduction in the roles of the banks in Japan and Germany). Yet, close as they are, these banking relations abroad may be less supportive of moves into the United States. Banking shifts have been lop-sided, with U.S. outward moves well outpacing foreign bank moves into the United States. This leaves foreign multinationals in the United States with little on-the-spot support by bankers familiar with the markets and the political setting. Such local roots are often decisive in giving firm guidance.[7]

The banking preconditions for a strong inward flow to the United States, then, are lacking. Entry barriers, a popular topic in analyzing U.S. industrial structure, may be important vis-à-vis international entry and may determine its outcome. A familiar barrier is the tariff or physical quota which keeps out imports. But presumably that would not influence take-overs or the building of new plants; indeed, it would be expected to stimulate them. Trade barriers, then, do not explain the small total volume of inward flow.

Perhaps there is a higher degree of risk in U.S. markets than in European or Japanese ones. There is always risk in moving from one culture to another: foreign management doesn't understand conditions as well; they may not be trusted or helped as much, and so foreign firms must expect more failures to occur in the wake of mistakes.

We also might define a class of conditions which in a sporting metaphor would be called the home-court advantage. The home court in this case involves not only U.S. companies operating in their own familiar markets, often with many decades of dominance, but also the whole set of U.S. policies, agencies, and processes. These include a great variety of officials, powers, and methods, by which an industry can secure an advantage for itself against virtually any new type of stress. For example, the firm can seek to change trade legislation and decisions. The Department of Commerce or some other group can be pressured to impose special conditions. Or a firm can work through the State Department against a potential or actual foreign competitor. There are many ways a U.S. company can seek to defend itself, not in the marketplace so much as through the political process. These methods are familiar through age-old usage, and we can expect them to be used in the future. Yet they have not worked widely for the Europeans and less developed countries in keeping American firms out.

How important will these home-court advantages be for U.S. firms? They obviously can be fairly strong in many cases. For instance, Iran is said to be assuming a major new role in Pan American Airway's ownership and control. But Iran is doing it with the very intimate involvement of the U.S. State Department, the C.A.B., and other agencies, dealing not only with permission per se but also working out the actual terms. Even closer scrutiny is likely to be applied in foreign takeovers of banks, weapons, producers, and also for any firm which can be portrayed as important or sensitive. This claim often powerfully activates state and federal legislators and executives. We can expect domestic firms to make it routinely any time they are threatened by foreign moves, and official reasons can usually be derived to justify excluding foreign control. In short, a wide range of official barriers can be invoked to stop moves inward by foreign firms. They may be more powerful than anything the Europeans have been able to mount against earlier moves outward by American firms.

Another possibility is that American firms are simply more fully able to threaten retaliation. Table 2 lists many such firms. They tend to be larger than their foreign counterparts; many of them are already operating extensively abroad: e.g., I.B.M., Coca-Cola, Procter & Gamble. They would be in a position to retaliate directly, and not only in the U.S. market. Therefore, we already have the preconditions for a diplomatic detente in which, if foreigners keep out of the United States, U.S. firms will avoid abusive behavior abroad. The classic retaliatory threat against a new entry or against a takeover attempt may be quite sufficient in many markets.

Finally it is possible that foreign firms simply are not interested. Many observers believe this is true of many British firms. Americans often exaggerate their own managerial excellence and professionalism, but U.S. firms may have a genuine degree of flexibility, skill, and international motivation beyond that of many foreign firms. The steel industry has been perhaps the main exception to this point; there a major innovation, the oxygen furnace, was overlooked by U.S. firms, and so foreign firms were given a rare, free opportunity. Japanese and German competition has been strong in a number of industries, but the conditions have shifted since 1970, so that the basis for moves into U.S. markets is less favorable. In both cases there have been serious economic problems at home. Both the Germans and the Japanese are more vulnerable to exchange-rate changes than had been thought in the past.

Because the research basis for analyzing these conditions is embryonic, any predictions are hazardous. Yet at this point a strong overseas base for moves into U.S. industries does not seem likely.

Are there any other technical factors that we might expect to affect this reverse flow? The sheer incentive for large gains in U.S. markets is one. But, although these gains could be large for medium-size firms seeking positions in large U.S. markets,[8] the actual results are often much less favorable. Consider two examples. One is Wilkinson Sword, Limited, which entered the U.S. razor blade market with a significant effect on Gillette's market position, profits, and stock price. When Wilkinson entered in the early 1960s as the first firm with a stainless steel blade, it did well. Gillette's market share went down sharply, and its stock price went down even more sharply. Yet Gillette quickly retaliated and has regained its position. Wilkinson is now only a minor factor. Another example is the Rolls Royce engine for the Lockhead RB 211. Winning that contract in 1968 against stiff opposition by U.S. companies (especially General Electric) and political groups was regarded as a major competitive inroad. Yet by 1971 it had bankrupted Rolls Royce and helped put Lockheed under great stress. Corporate officers who were knighted in 1969 were fired in 1971.

Perhaps the risks and outcomes in these two cases were strictly peculiar. Yet the episodes illustrate the limits on entry by outsiders. They can apply genuine pressure and gain large temporary advantages, but to establish lasting market shares and to change behavior markedly is much more difficult. Despite the inducements, the inward moves are usually slight.

Economies of scale could be an additional stimulus to inward moves. If foreign firms, which are usually smaller than their U.S. counterparts, could gain positions in U.S. markets, they might be able to achieve really striking scale economies. This would generate high profitability and rapid rises in market shares. Unfortunately for the validity of this hypothesis, the more recent, thorough studies give it little support. For the broad range of industries in Europe, economies of scale are generally realized well within the size of the domestic markets. Therefore, leading firms in these industries have little extra impetus to seek foreign sales, either by exporting to the United States or by moving parts of their companies to the United States.

On the whole, we must admit that there are few strong economic factors likely to cause foreign firms to reverse the old shifts and move into the target industries in the United States. Such a process may occur randomly by accident, or because of personality or new broad upheavals. Rather than an abundance of inward moves, it is wise to expect only a limited and uneven flow.

Policy Issues

Are there any policy lessons to be drawn? Apparently the reverse flow is not going to be a broad process of self-correction in which major pockets of market power in the United States are going to attract new competition or takeover from abroad. The flow may strongly influence a few areas, as steel and automobile producers already know. But even if we strain to keep all artificial barriers down, the process is not likely to do away with most – or perhaps very much at all – of our core problems of market power. Still, and perhaps especially *because* no broad intrusion seems imminent, it is efficient to preserve whatever there is of a corrective effect from foreign multinationals. The world is made up of a lot of little things, and this moderate effect would be well worth having.

The possibility of takeovers is especially interesting. There is likely to be a moderate, if not large, volume of foreign investible funds, including Arabian oil money, which may seek outlets in established western firms. The early reactions to this in Germany, the United States, and elsewhere have been unstable and negative. Instead, most such take-over attempts should be treated neutrally or even encouraged. Large flows of so-called surplus petro-dollars are likely to go into Swiss bank accounts and other passive forms, such as portfolio holdings; any take-over action, therefore, is likely to be on a modest scale. Moreover it can be blocked in many ways by firms using political devices for self-protection.

Perhaps our main task in this area is to advise against such exclusionary actions. New, outside competitors and interests can have a tonic effect on a number of monopolistic industries. They will face disadvantages, and have to contend with U.S. banks which are the advisors and allies of many of the U.S. companies involved, and they will have to reckon with U.S. policy. We must be sure to define the public interest carefully, lest we be overpersuaded that it is identical with the claims of the U.S. firms in the target industries. The signs point to a biased reaction against these moderate new forces, rather than a neutral one.

The issues are not clear-cut, and some inward moves can pose valid problems of sovereignty and domestic interest. Yet a new shift toward some inward move by foreign firms and finance can be beneficial, in the long tradition of *harmoniedoctrine*. This will also comport with the longer-term adjustment of the United States as part of a balanced world economic community.

Notes

1. See Raymond Vernon, *Sovereignty at Bay* (New York: Basic Books, 1971); Rainer Hellmann, *The Challenge of U.S. Dominance of the International Corporation* (New York: Dunellen, 1970); and various studies by John H. Dunning.

2. See the pathbreaking paper by Richard E. Caves, *International Trade, International Investment, and Imperfect Markets,* Special Papers in International Economics, No. 10 (Princeton, N.J.: Department of Economics, Princeton University, Nov. 1974) and the references he cites there.

3. See Caves, *International Trade . . .*

4. See W.G. Shepherd, "The Elements of Market Structure," *Review of Economics and Statistics,* Feb. 1972, pp. 25-37, and *The Treatment of Market Power* (New York: Columbia University Press, 1975).

5. This question is explored at length in my *Treatment of Market Power.*

6. The general effect of such losses of market share is also strong; see *Treatment.*

7. See Martin Mayer, *The Bankers* (New York: Weybright and Talley, 1974) for an account of some of these problems.

8. The yields to market share are indeed substantial; see my "Elements."

PREVIOUS VOLUMES IN THIS SERIES

The Future of Economic Policy, Myron H. Ross, Editor, 1966
Michigan Business Papers, No. 44, 1967

Paul W. McCracken	*The Political Position of the Council of Economic Advisers*
Robert Eisner	*Fiscal and Monetary Policy for Economic Growth*
Theodore W. Schultz	*Public Approaches to Minimize Poverty*
Jesse W. Markham	*Antitrust Policy after a Decade of Vigor*
Kenneth E. Boulding	*The Price System and the Price of the Great Society*
Robert Triffin	*International Monetary Reform*

Key Factors in Economic Growth, Raymond E. Zelder, Editor, 1967
Michigan Business Papers, No. 48, 1968

Martin Bronfenbrenner	*Japanese Economic Development in the Meiji Era, 1867-1912*
Nicholas Spulber	*Is the U.S.S.R. Going Capitalist?*
Milos Samardzija	*Economic Growth and Workers' Management in Yugoslavia*
Lauchlin Currie	*The Crisis in Latin American Development*
Edmundo Flores	*The Alliance for Progress and the Mexican Revolution*
Alexander Eckstein	*The Economic Development of Communist China*

The Cost of Conflict, John A. Copps, Editor, 1968
Michigan Business Papers, No. 51, 1969

Kenneth E. Boulding	*The Threat System*
Thomas C. Schelling	*The Diplomacy of Violence*
Seymour Melman	*The Price of Peace*
Murray L. Weidenbaum	*Towards a Peacetime Economy*
Roger E. Bolton	*National Defense and Regional Development*
Emile Benoit	*Economic Adjustments to Peace in the Far East and to Ending the Arms Race*

America's Cities, Wayland D. Gardner, Editor, 1969
Michigan Business Papers, No. 54, 1970

Wilbur R. Thompson	*The Process of Metropolitan Development: American Experience*
Hugh O. Nourse	*Industrial Location and Land Use in Metropolitan Areas*
Richard F. Muth	*The Economics of Slum Housing*
Dick Netzer	*Urban Government Finance and Urban Development*
Werner Z. Hirsch	*The Urban Challenge to Governments*

Antitrust Policy and Economic Welfare, Werner Sichel, Editor, 1970
Michigan Business Papers, No. 56, 1970

Walter Adams	*The Case for a Comprehensive and Vigorous Antitrust Policy*
Jules Backman	*Holding the Reins on the Trust Busters*
Almarin Phillips	*Antitrust Policies: Could They Be Tools of the Establishment?*
Richard B. Heflebower	*The Conglomerate in American Industry: A Special Antitrust Wrinkle*
Jesse W. Markham	*Structure versus Conduct Criteria in Antitrust*
William G. Shepherd	*Changing Contrasts in British and American Antitrust Policies*

Economic Policies in the 1970s, Akfred K. Ho, Editor, 1971
Michigan Business Papers, No. 57, 1971

James M. Buchanan	*Economists, the Government, and the Economy*
Martin Bronfenbrenner	*Nixonomics and Stagflation Reconsidered*
David I. Fand	*Some Observations on Current Stabilization Policy*
Gardner Ackley	*International Inflation*
Harry G. Johnson	*Inflation: A "Monetarist" View*
Bela Balassa	*Prospects and Problems of British Entry into the Common Market*

The Economics of Environmental Problems, Frank C. Emerson, Editor, 1972
Michigan Business Papers, No. 58, 1973

Joseph L. Fisher	*An Introduction to Environmental Economics*
Lester B. Lave	*The Economic Costs of Air Pollution*
Robert H. Haveman	*The Political Economy of Federal Water Quality Policy*
William S. Vickery	*The Economics of Congestion Control in Urban Transportation*
Jerome Rothenberg	*The Evaluation of Alternative Public Policy Approaches to Environmental Control*

The Economics of Education, Myron H. Ross, Editor, 1973
Michigan Business Papers, No. 59, 1974

Charles C. Killingsworth	*The Evaluation of Manpower Programs*
Samuel Bowles	*The Integration of Higher Education into the Wage-Labor System*
Richard Eckaus	*How Much and What Kinds of Education for Economic Development?*
Theodore W. Schultz	*Investments in Ourselves: Opportunities and Implications*
Jerry Miner	*Methods of Finance and the Organization and Administration of Local Schools*

The U.S. Medical Care Industry, Joseph C. Morreale, Editor, 1974
Michigan Business Papers, No. 60, 1974

Paul Feldstein	*The Present Medical Care System in the United States: An Economic Problem*
Harry Schwartz	*The Case for American Medicine*
Gerald Rosenthal	*Health Service Research, Health Policy, and the Real World*
Donald E. Yett	*An Economic Analysis of the Market for Nurses*
Reuben A. Kessel	*The Role of Organized Medicine in Determining our Health Care System*
Herbert E. Klarman	*What Kind of Health Insurance Should the United States Choose?*